Frances Parker Laughton Mace

Legends, Lyrics, and Sonnets

Frances Parker Laughton Mace

Legends, Lyrics, and Sonnets

ISBN/EAN: 9783741183782

Manufactured in Europe, USA, Canada, Australia, Japa

Cover: Foto ©Thomas Meinert / pixelio.de

Manufactured and distributed by brebook publishing software
(www.brebook.com)

Frances Parker Laughton Mace

Legends, Lyrics, and Sonnets

LEGENDS

LYRICS AND SONNETS

BY

FRANCES L. MACE

BOSTON

CUPPLES, UPHAM AND COMPANY

𝔒𝔩𝔡 𝔠𝔬𝔯𝔫𝔢𝔯 𝔅𝔬𝔬𝔨𝔰𝔱𝔬𝔯𝔢

1883

CONTENTS.

LEGENDS.

LYRICS.

SONNETS

LEGENDS.

LEGENDS.

ISRAFIL.

ISRAFIL!
Stay thy sickle on vale and hill.
Come from the woods whose gorgeous leaves
Pale and wither beneath thy tread :
Come from binding among thy sheaves
Dearer blossoms of beauty dead,
Of grandeur and of worth
Wrested away from earth.
Bend thy sorrowful eyes on me,
Angel of death ! and while nature breathes
One hour from thy sad dominion free,
Tell me the mystery of thy woe,
The legend I only have heard in dreams.
Over my heart shall flow

In fuller measures the solemn strain,
Up from depths of tears and pain
Rising to patience, — rising again
To a pæan of triumph.
                                    Hush! be still!

Whence this odor of amaranth wreaths?
Whence these faint and starlike beams
Shed from feet which make no sound?
A touch of fire
Is on my lyre,
And its strings with a sudden, rapturous, bound
Thrill beneath the angel fingers.
Thou art come — thou art gone!
Yet in all my being lingers
A breath celestial, a voiceless tone, —
I shall not utter my song alone,
Israfil!

On Paradise
A softer hue of glory lies,
The hush of evening, for the night
Comes slowly o'er young Eden's skies,
Reluctant to conceal from sight
One blossom's radiant dyes.
A thousand birds amid the shade,
To sleep their shining plumage fold,

A thousand flowers that cannot fade
Perfume afresh their leaves of gold,
Far off, rising stars illume
The gentle, yet half fearful gloom
Which folds in deeper shade yon myrtle bower.
There lost in slumbers pure and deep,
Wrapt in the stillness of the hour,
Unconscious yet of tempter's power,
The first-born, guiltless mortals sleep.

Lo! down the airy waste
Four shining angels haste :
Their eager wings make music as they come,
Flashing along the night,
All redolent of light,
As if the splendors of their upper home
Reflected still illumed their earthward flight.
On, swiftly on, past star by star,
Leaving a path of glory far
Behind their luminous wings, at last
The measureless expanse is past,
And at their feet in beauty lies
The new-made, earthly Paradise.
As when from envious shadow breaks
Sweet Hesperus and walks the aisles
Of heaven's blue temple, nature smiles
And added grace and beauty takes,

So Eden, conscious in its dreams
Of a diviner atmosphere,
Breathes richer fragrance far and near,
And in the angelic presence beams.

A moment stay their steps to view
Scenes to angel vision new, —
Roses burdened with the dew
By the tender night distilled,
Birds whose last good-night is trilled
Sleeping on the tremulous bough,
Fountains white in moonlight glow :
But a moment, for the night
Deepens, and without the gate
Evil spirits hide and wait.
Each bright angel seeks his post,
Armed, and mightier than a host
Of the envious, guileful band
That in outer darkness stand.
Northward, southward, westward go
One by one the heavenly guard,
Clothed about with garments white
That diffuse a silvery glow,
Bearing each a sword of light
With celestial jewels starred.
Last with lingering steps that seem
Loth to seek the nightly stand

On the utmost eastern hill,
Youngest of the angel band,
Lovelier than a poet's dream,
Comes the angel Israfil!

Now quicker in his noiseless tread,
His silvery wings expanding spread,
Half floats he in the air with deep delight
As scenes of new enchantment meet his sight.
His eyes of liquid azure, touched with fire,
More beautiful than can be sung or told,
Shine 'neath the aureole of his locks of gold,
With a soft restlessness, a fond desire.
Adoring beauty with a love
Too passionate for one of angel birth,
Even at this hour he pants to rove
Amid the green bowers of the fragrant earth;
To hear once more the nightingale's refrain,
To touch the humid, sleeping rose again,
But most of all to see
The latest miracle of Deity, —
The revelation, unto angels new,
Of loveliness they scarcely yet conceive
As real, substantial, true,
The first of human womanhood,
The breathing form, the spirit pure and good,
The garden's royal flower, the new created Eve.

O Israfil !
Bid thy impulsive soul be still,
Until the morning wait !
Leave not the haunted gate
Where even now, by evil sense aware
Of thy untried and hasty mood,
The serpent King with envious hate
Whispers, to tempt thy angelhood,
Of her the wonderfully fair,
Whom but to look upon would be
A rapture and an ecstasy.
O Israfil,
Keep well thy watch upon the starlit hill,
Until the morning wait !
Then when the summons from on high
Recalls thy comrades to the sky,
She shall come forth, and with sweet converse
    greet
The parting and the coming angel host.
Stay thy impetuous feet ;
One moment now absented from thy post,
And all is lost.
The serpent watches well : thou shalt return too
    late !

An hour is past,
All Eden sleeps in motionless repose.

Around, above, he casts his restless eyes
And sighs to think how long the night will last.
The moon rides slowly, slowly down the skies.
Surely far off have vanished Eden's foes.
No evil spirit can be lurking near,
No sound, no breath meets his attentive ear.
So long the night, so deep the silence grows,
May he not wander at his wayward will
If not too distant from the sentinel hill?
Only a few light steps will bring him near
The bower of which the angels oft have told.
There in the moonlight clear
A moment tarrying, he may behold,
And seeing may believe
That only he has learned how beautiful is Eve.

As now with wilful steps he seeks
The bower where she is slumbering,
The dew brushed by his rapid wing
From hanging boughs, falls on his cheeks.
His feet are trampling in their haste
The straying rose, a wildwood vine
Whose flowers the mossy pathway graced.
He starts, when in the bright moonshine
A bird, awakened, trills a note,
Then sleeps, the song still rippling from his
    throat.

But soon he trembles, listens, doubts no more:
All else forgotten he is bending o'er
The violet bed, amid whose blest perfume
Earth's fairest being sleeps, unconscious of her
    doom.

She sleeps — she dreams —
For now a smile hovers with tender grace
About her lips.   The beauty of her face
A breathing wonder to the angel seems.
Her dark eyelashes rest
Motionless on the warm flush of her cheek,
Her lips part softly, as if she would speak
But had in dreamland lost the word she fain
    would seek!
One hand is lightly clasped about a rose
Which fully open blows,
Too blest to share its sister flowers' repose.
And veiling her white breast
Falls wave on wave of lustrous golden hair.
Like one enchanted in the moonlight glow,
The angel lingers still and murmurs low,
"Daughter of earth, how fair!"

Israfil!   Israfil!
The cry rings through the startled night.
The angels speed in sudden fright

Toward the unprotected gate.
On wings of fear flies Israfil —
Alas! he flies too late.
His brother angels flashing by
Already with pure sense perceive
An evil lurking nigh.
A change comes o'er the moonlit sky:
The wind begins to sigh and grieve;
The garden feels a sudden chill, —
The breath of coming fate.
" Where hast thou strayed, O Israfil?
The serpent's taint is on the air.
The son of darkness, once as fair
And frail as thou, is come!"
He hides his face in his despair
And stands before them, dumb.

All night the angels to and fro
Seek for the messenger of woe.
He, subtle, silent, still eludes
Their search. In densest solitudes
Evades the lustre that is shed
From their celestial tread.
At morn, recalled, they seek the skies,
But Israfil with drooping wings
No longer heavenward can arise,
To earth unwilling clings.

Through all that fateful day, hour after hour,
With deepest sorrow thrilled,
He stands invisible, apart,
Sees evil warring with the human heart,
And Eden's doom fulfilled.
When in the evening cool the Lord appears,
Sees the forbidden tree with broken bloom,
The garden desolate and lost in gloom,
The mortals hiding from his searching gaze,
Israfil, speechless, hears
Their fate pronounced, sees their repentant
　　tears
And death's dread shadow hanging o'er their
　　days.
And now on him the rays
Of the Eternal Vision fall, the word
Of his own doom is heard.
"Since death by thee is come unto the earth,
Be thou its messenger. Thy name shall be
A terror unto all of human birth;
The shadow of the grave forever follow thee."

In Eden it was early dawn.
How changed since in the even-time
The angel saw it in its prime.
The erring mortals now were gone:
He stood within their empty bower alone.

Above his head
A little bird was warbling cheerily.
The music mocked his speechless misery.
He raised his hand, unconscious of his power,
And grasped the bough which held the dainty nest,
And the branch shrivelled in his hand; with
    breast
Panting in sudden pain, the bird fell dead.
Aghast, he seized a flower, —
The rose which Eve's fair hand at night had
    pressed;
Beneath his touch it withered; bud and leaf
Dropped dry and scentless. In a bitter grief
He murmured — "This is death!
And this henceforth shall be my destiny, —
To slay but not to die.
To blight all things of mortal breath,
All earthly loveliness to sere,
All that yon beings hold most dear
Must perish when my steps draw near.
Nor can I shun my fearful power,
Or spare from them one dreaded hour.
Onward I go through all the years,
Unheeding human prayers and tears.
Let mortals seek through toil and fears
Some transient gleams of love and joy,
I follow after to destroy."

" Israfil! "
The angel looked and bowed his face
Before a brow whose sweet, majestic grace
Had shone upon him oft in happier morn,
From the Eternal hill
Whose dazzling height reveals the Father's
    throne.
Immanuel the First Born
Stood smiling on him in the early dawn.
" Israfil, behold ! "
The Son takes in his hand the withered rose,
Its petals seem like magic to unfold.
A new, celestial bloom,
A heavenly perfume
Through the awakened blossom breathes and
    glows.
The Savior smiling lays it on His breast.
He takes the dead bird from its broken nest, —
It flutters, plumes its wings,
Then rapturously sings
And soars away toward the beaming Heaven.
Then spake He — " Israfil,
The Father to the Son a boon hath given.
Go forth, but I am with thee.   Do His will
Who laid this doom upon thee, and be still.
Thou dost destroy, but thus can I restore.
Angel of death arise, and hope once more !

From Abel's blood spilt on the altar stone
To Calvary's cross which I must bear alone,
Thou shalt be terrible to human kind
And hope but dimly light the troubled mind.
But from that grave which yields to me its
        portal,
Faith shall come forth, the Comforter immortal,
And thou, new-crowned, shalt be
Seen by believing eyes linked hand in hand with
        Me!"

Thus spake Immanuel, and ascending passed
Again unto His Father's house, to keep
Unbroken watch while time and sorrow last,
Of His beloved who in death shall sleep.
And Israfil arose, serene and calm,
And with one last look upon Eden's bower,
Went forth into the morning's fragrant balm,
To wield forevermore his melancholy power.

Israfil!
Let thy sickle return to the harvest that gleams
White and wan on valley and hill,
For my lyre is still.
The song that I heard in the land of dreams
Is sung, and its magic shall haunt me no more.
Ever yet to the unseen shore

Bear earth's harvest, the loved and lost.
Often thy shadow my door has crossed.
I have seen thy icy fingers laid
On lips that I loved and was not afraid.
Following close on thy chill and gloom,
Reaching up from the darkened tomb
Was the very odor of heavenly bloom
Shed from His garments who followed thee,
And took my idols to keep for me.

Israfil!
Come again at the Master's will.
At thy cross and pang my flesh may shrink,
But thy bitter cup I will dare to drink,
And follow thee down to the river's brink.
Through the breathless tide
I will cling to the hand of the Crucified.
And when I awake on the further shore
I shall see thee no more
Sad and shrouded in garments dim,
But the angel of peace, and brother of Him
Who crowned thee and blessed thee on Cal-
　　'vary's Hill,
Israfil!

HESPERUS.

Awake, O beautiful Hesperus!
 Awake! for the day is done,
And the royal purple curtains are drawn
 Round the couch of the sleeping sun.
There is a hush on the blooming earth,
 A hush on the beating sea,
And silence, too, in the courts of Heaven,
 For the stars all wait for thee,
  Hesperus!
All things beautiful wait for thee.

Tis the hour for fancy's fairy reign,
 When the glowing brain is fraught
With visions of beauty and bliss and love
 That leave no room for thought.
With the light of warm and glorious dreams
 This narrow chamber is bright,
And I need but thee to sing with me,
 O sweetest poet of night!
  Hesperus,
Open thy volume of golden light.

15

There may I read of the youth of old
  Who clambered the mountain height,
And talked with stars in the midnight hours
  Till he faded from human sight.
Till his brow grew bright with wonderful light,
  And away from the world's rude jars,
He was lost in the beams of his radiant dreams
  And himself was the fairest of stars.
        Hesperus!
The best beloved of all the stars!

There may I read this legend rare
  And its beautiful meaning learn,
While my soul new kindled to hopes divine
  With a holy fire shall burn.
O never should human heart despair
  Of the presence of God on high,
O never should human faith grow dim,
  While the stars are in the sky!
        Hesperus,
Thy voice is the voice of eternity.

Thou art smiling down on me, Hesperus!
  With that smile upon my heart
I know that kindred to me and mine
  In those measureless heights thou art.

When thy spirit blossomed into a star
  In the mystical days of old,
The love and the hope it bore on high,
  The legend hath never told.
      Hesperus,
Thy sweetest story hath never been told.

O to be like thee, Hesperus!
  To climb the heights of truth,
And there to drink of celestial airs,
  To glow with immortal youth;
There wrapt in the light which is born in skies
  Where the blessed angels are,
To hear earth's harmonies only rise,
  Floating sweetly up from afar.
      Hesperus!
How can my spirit be made a star?

A LEGEND OF THE DAWN.

From a bed of velvet the Tourmaline
Its crystal splendors of red and green,
Toned and mellowed by milk-white bars,
Flashed in the sunset. The prisoned rays
Glittering, shimmering under my gaze,
Now soft as the rainbow's melting haze,
Now fierce and fine as the light of stars,
Held me, thrilled me with magic glance!
All the fairest and wildest flights
Of fancy, winged in Arabian Nights,
Circling slow in bewildering dance
Seemed to float o'er the jewel rare.
Till half afraid, lest a look profane
The spell-bound spirit imprisoned there,
I turned away, — but all in vain —
The mystery breathed from the page again.

For there I read of pure and priceless ores
Stored as by some malignant, fateful plan,
In desert isles, on solitary shores,
Beyond the reach and far from haunts of man.

18

Of wrath of winds and waters, storm and fire
To baffle and to thwart the world's desire
For precious stones; and though with new
    delight
Age after age some treasure brings to sight,
Brilliants unnumbered sleep in endless night.
In secret still the jealous elements nurse
The crystal blossoms of the universe.

I closed the book. I lifted from its bed
Of tawny velvet the enchanted stone.
Again its fiery glance upon me shone,
All sense of present, actual being fled.
Backward, far backward in the dawn of time
Floated my vision; in creation's prime,
When Genii roamed in daring strength abroad,
But living souls were hidden still with God.

Can this be morning, — this light which breaks
In utter silence o'er land and sea?
No bower in the forest, no tent on the lea,
No sail on the rivers, no oar on the lakes,
Nor voice, nor motion of grief or glee?
Even the sunlight, a languid ray,
Lingers and dreams at the door of day.
But hark! what tone, what elfin strain
Wakens the landscape to life again?

"Come Genii of the deep!
Come, giant forms of the earth and sky!
Ye who toil without rest or sleep,
Whose lips never smile and whose eyes never
weep,
But whose hands are mighty to gather and reap
The beautiful harvest of diadems.
Come, for the end of your toil is nigh.
The days primeval are told;
The veins of the earth are full of gold;
The ocean's sparkling floor
Lights up the waters with glittering ore,
Over vast spaces like shadows creep,
And come to the island of gems."

A voice like music wafted from afar,
Faint and aërial and unreal as are
The utterances of all the soulless things
Which of mysterious birth
Move to and fro upon the living earth,
Sent forth this wild and melancholy call.
It floated out upon the winds, and all
The breezy spirits spread their fragrant wings
And bore it up and down the sea and land.
It pierced the depths, and drowsy ocean stirred
And sounded it again, till it was heard
In deepest cave, on farthest icy strand.

Then to the island of flame
Luminous far over tropic seas,
Summoned by heralds of billow and breeze,
Unnumbered Genii came.
Gem of the ocean the island lay,
Veiled with a mist of rainbow spray ;
Nor leaf, nor verdure adorned the side
Of the sloping cliffs, but far and wide
Crystal masses of white and green,
Beds of amethyst, paths of spar
Spangled with diamonds brighter far
Than noonday's radiant sunbeams are ;
Terrace of rubies, like scarlet flowers,
Sapphire violets, emerald bowers,
Crimson and olive tourmaline,
With banks of topaz whose azure gleams
Were blent with pearl wreaths of silver sheen.
Hither swiftly and silently came
Spirits of billow and vapor and flame,
Subject all to the beautiful queen
          Eola of golden beams !

She solitary on her brilliant throne,
A seat of gold with vivid gems inwrought —
Beheld them as they gathered one by one.
Each to her feet some sparkling jewel brought,
Which with new lustre in her presence shone.

Giants were they in form, and dark and grave,
Their features neither hope nor sorrow wore;
In time's first hours to them the Maker gave
Such endless life as earthly elements have,
With strength and will to work the precious ore.
Arrayed before the sovereign, as in turn
Her shining glance on each one chanced to burn,
The shadow brings, dusky, dark and stern
Gave forth prismatic lights of various hue,
Till like their own rich handiwork they grew.

" Ye to whom power is given
Over the secrets of land and sea,
Mingling the life-giving beams of heaven
With the dark vapors, the deathly mould
That earth's abysses and caverns hold,
Into the night of memory reach!
Borrow of winds and waters speech,
            And tell once more
The work ye have wrought with the shining ore."

Then one who spake for many, bowed him low
Before her throne.   "Eola! thou dost know
We were of Chaos and of Darkness born.
Without thee we were helpless, blind and weak.
But when the first Day grew to glowing morn,
Daughter of Light! thy glance had power to speak

Our torpor into life. By thee sent forth,
Armed with thy beams, we wandered south and
    north
And to remotest wilds of east and west,
The purest treasure of the earth our quest.
Where'er thy spear on desert rock or land
Revealed a grain of unpolluted sand,
Lustrous and clear, we bore it to the strand
Of mighty ocean, and the salt sea wave
Planted in priceless beds the seed we gave.
Flames wrought beneath the ocean, central fires
Upturned the depths, and laid on every shore
Perfected miracles of precious ore.
Now we rejoice in thy fulfilled desires."

    Then hastily bending down,
    One laid at her feet a crown
From whose central jewel seemed to unfurl
Petals of opal with frosts of pearl,
And sprays like dew-drops on yellow sheaves.
"The light of thy love, O queen!
We have wrought into brilliants of purple and
    green,
Into blossoms that never shall lose their sheen,
Nor their glowing, beautiful dyes.
Each glance of thy sunny eyes
Some happy spirit delighted weaves

Into deathless beauty.   Let thy command
Speed on our labors.   From every land
Let us bring the spoil, till the final day
The reign of the human shall end our sway."·

As some fair tree white with perfected bloom
Waves slowly to and fro, and slowly fall
The snowflake petals, till the verdure all
Is strewn with drifts of prodigal perfume,
So now Eola, sun-born spirit, shook
Her waving tresses with a mournful smile,
And falling beams illumined all the isle.
"That day has come, O genii! ye may look
Even now upon the new created one
For whom all days their wonder work have done.
My spirits, do ye not remember well
When from the vast, blue dome above, there fell
A Voice which shook the firmament, and ye
Heard the Invisible utter His decree —
"Let us make man!" the angels heard and sung
Pæans with which the whirling planets rung,
But in the deepest shade
Ye hid yourselves, sore troubled and afraid.
O Genii! know that unto the last day
Of the creation only, we have sway.
The world is ripe for man; we phantoms must
     away!"

Then sounds and sighings of woe
Through all the island were heard,
And the waves of the listening ocean stirred
And beat on the fringing coral reef
With a sullen, angry flow,
And an undertone of grief.
"Ah! we remember, queen!
We too have the omens seen
Of creation's ultimate change.
It was not for us that the waters rolled
And left the isles and continents free.
It was not for us that verdure and tree,
Foliage gorgeous and manifold,
With flowers like jewels of red and gold, —
Robed the valleys and wreathed the hills;
Not ours the shadow of oak and palm,
And fruits that ripen with breath of balm;
Not ours the music the wild bird trills
Nor the strength of the forest.
　　　　　But say, O queen,
What later signal thine eyes have seen."

Slowly she spoke — the shining lustre shed
In fainter sparkles from her beaming head.
"I saw, O children of the fire and flood,
A garden which your feet have never trod.

Vast, beautiful and rich with foliage rare,
Earth has no vale so spacious nor so fair.
And in the midst one walked, of lesser height
Than we, but firm, compact, and fair to sight.
He spoke — his voice rang out distinct and clear;
The beasts with mild obedience drew near,
And the birds hushed their delicate notes to
     hear.
I glided closer and by him unseen
Watched his superior step, his fearless mien,
Until with brow uplifted to the sky
He said aloud ' Our Father ! ' from on high
The Voice that called the days to life replied,
And I fled trembling from the garden's side.
Alas! in fearful haste I dropped a gem,
The brightest star from out my diadem,
Low at his feet it lies,
Mocked by the fairer bloom of Paradise.

" But not for the new born race
Are the treasures that ye have won
My children of fire and sun !
Still in some secret space,
Some hidden grotto of earth or cave,
In mountain granite or black sea wave
We will find a resting-place.

To your utmost depths ye sons of fire!
Ye foam-tressed waves roll wilder, higher,
Snow spirits, winds, your plumes outspread,
Daughters of sunlight o'er wide earth flee —
And wherever a mortal foot may tread,
Gather in haste and bring to me.
We will bury our jewels in mountain and main,
And the mighty, hereafter, shall seek them in
    vain."

Silent and swift the genii now began
To hide the riches they had wrought, from man.
Into great rifts of mountain rock they poured
The gold a thousand centuries had stored,
With gleaming sands the river beds were sown.
Masses of crystal, violet, rose, and white,
Tinting the waters far with colored light,
Into the secret ocean depths were thrown.
Hard was their toil, nor did Eola shun
To give them aid, though daughter of the sun.
At sunset all was ended. Gathered there
Upon the island desolate and bare,
Dim, wavering forms already fain to flee
The presence of unknown humanity,
They looked upon their queen. She took her
    crown,
Of its lost gem despoiled, and cast it down

Into the waters. From her shoulders fell
The mantle of the sunbeams. "Now, farewell,
Sweet light of day!" she uttered — "We will
    keep
Eternal watch within the unsounded deep.
Woe to the hand that for the prize may dare
In toil and pain to search. The rock shall be
Of adamantine strength : the trusty sea
Unwilling yield one golden grain, and care
And ill unmeasured be the victor's share."

Fading, fading away,
Lost in the dying day,
The Genii vanished from sea and shore.
Loudly lamented the winds ; the sun
Sunk among vapors ashy and dun,
The rain-clouds sobbed as the night begun,
The island trembled and quaked with woe.
There were sounds of feet going to and fro
On the ocean's echoing floor,
But moaning tempest, nor midnight rain,
Nor morning sunlight could call again
The Genii forth. With charm and sign
They had touched each gem of their boundless
    store,
The door was sealed of each golden mine,
The pathway darkened forevermore.

THE BIRTH OF THE ROSE.

Long ago a lovely wood nymph,
  Flora's fairest child,
Roamed Arcadia's velvet meadows,
  Silent, shy, and wild,

Until Death, enamored, met her
  In her beauty's glow,
Touched her with his lip of marble,
  Kissed her cheek to snow.

Flora found her 'mid the blossoms
  Beautiful and still.
"Help!" she cried, "ye happy dwellers
  On the purple hill!

"Wrest from Death the fairest being
  Ever missed from earth;
Let the flower of nymphs inherit
  A celestial birth."

See the shining ones descending!
  All Arcadia gleams.

First Apollo warms her forehead
  With electric beams:

Bacchus bathes her lips with nectar
  Worthy of the god:
Her white feet Vertumnus covers
  With a fragrant sod.

Lo! the radiant transformation!
  One by one unclose
Tendrils, leaves, and snowy petals
  Of the perfect Rose!

All the nymph's remembered graces
  Hover round the flower,
Sweetness, tenderness, and passion
  Still her beauty's dower.

Soon the praise of the Immortals
  To a richer flush
Warms the rose — her colors brighten
  To Aurora's blush;

Then the nightingale in rapture
  Warbles sweet and long
Till a hue of love's vermilion
  Answers to his song.

" Bloom forever nymph enchanted!"
  The Olympians cry —
" Kindred both to earth and heaven,
  Thou shalt never die!"

Down through centuries of blossom,
  Ages of delight,
Still the royal rose of summer
  Opens on our sight.

And the half-bewildered fancy
  Through the fragrant bowers
Searches for the haunting mystery
  Of this flower of flowers.

'T is the nymph so deftly hidden
  In a leafy shrine,
In her golden heart still throbbing
  Memories divine.

Ever silent, ever seeing,
  Every heart she knows, —
All thy love, thy hope, thy longing
  Whisper to the Rose!

BALDUR THE BEAUTIFUL.

In the far north, when the midsummer night
Is but the sunset wedded to the light
Of a new morning, upon cliff and hill
Burns the bale-fire to Baldur: as its flame
Salutes the sleepless sun, the Norsemen still
      Utter that sacred name,
And year by year the wonder-myth is told
Of Baldur, joy of men and gods in days of old!

   On royal Asgard's height
No god like Baldur beamed upon the sight.
Others were mighty, — he was pure as light.
Pleasant his voice as rivulets, his eyes
Sun bright and radiant as midsummer skies,
  And his long yellow locks gave forth perfumes
When the wind-giant shook with glee his eagle
    plumes.

All living things adored him. Singing birds
Their joyance caught from listening to his
    words,

Flames, floods, winds, lightnings, in accordant
    breath
Vowed that to him should come no stroke of
    death.
The orcs and rocks, the mosses, vines, and trees,
    The strong, tumultuous seas
Gave glad response, and it was sung and said
By all the beams above, the shades below,
The snow-white feet of Baldur ne'er should
    tread
    The path of wail and woe
Down to the ice-walled dwelling of the dead.
One thing alone was dumb, — *the creeping
    mistletoe!*

Thus in no fear of death, the gods at play
Made him their target, while the midnight sun
Smiled o'er the wide, pale moors with mellow
    ray,
    Half evening and half day,
And Baldur lightly caught and tossed away
Sword, lance, or arrow, till with victories won
His brow grew dazzling, and the farthest fields
Of Asgard were illumined, and the shields
Upon Valhalla with his image shone.
    Then stepped the blind old god
Höder upon the arrow-sprinkled sod ;

He too would share the merriment. Ah! woe!
To Baldur's heart sped straight the fated
   mistletoe!

Beautiful as a marble god he lay,
   When life had ebbed away,
Or like a rose tree in its prime cut down
   With all its flowery crown.
Time never knew a more despairing cry
   Than smote the startled sky.
It reached the utmost depths of death and
   night,
And Hela, goddess terrible to sight,
   Trembled upon her throne,
And gazed on the white ghost she dared not call
   her own.

But swift a messenger had followed him,
   And at the portals grim
Knocked loud. "What ransom, Hela, shall
   be given
By heroes of the earth and gods of Heaven,
To win beloved Baldur back to life?
Already discord mutters sounds of strife
And clouds of vengeance gather. Speak and
   take
The wealth of land and ocean for his sake!"

And as Valhalla's message borne above
The mists of Nifflehem, on wings of love,
Reached Hela's seat, with sudden pity moved,
She spoke — "If Baldur was so greatly loved,
Bid all the world to weep; the heart-wrung
    moan
Of every living thing may melt Death's heart
    of stone."

The wide world heard and with a rain of tears
Gave answer, but in all the countless years
Baldur returns not, and no later skies
Have smiled upon his vanished Paradise.
Though the soft falling dews bring new-born
    day
      With fresh, alluring ray,
The winter frosts dissolve in penitent grief
      And open bud and leaf,
Baldur the Beautiful takes not his place
Fairest of human as of godlike race,
Earth has not tears enough to bring again
Lost innocence, pure peace, — Heaven's primal

THE GARDEN OF IREM.

WHERE burns beneath Arabia's dazzling sky
    The desert waste of Aden, leafless, bare,
    A stately garden on the Elysian air
Its beauty shed, entrancing every eye.
        An oasis of green,
Brilliant with flowers and silvery waters' sheen.

The fig and olive yielded fragrant shade,
    The vine with royal purple decked the wall;
    Sweet was the music of the fountain's fall,
Whose dancing drops among the roses played,
        And all the balmy night
The bulbul trilled his tremulous delight.

A palace in the midst arose, whose towers
    The sunshine mocked with gilded opulence,
    Its inner court reflected rays intense,
Inlaid with gems that sparkled 'mid the flowers.
        Through glistening wires of gold,
Birds rainbow-hued their plaintive numbers told.

36

The doors were ever open, and the sound
  Of ceaseless mirth made day most musical,
  Never was heard the trumpet's warning call,
For feast and pageant led the year around.
    Till Irem's happy name
The symbol of terrestrial bliss became.

Then suddenly — while yet the warbling lute
  Vibrated to the dancer's jewelled feet,
  The Simoom of the desert, fierce and fleet,
Swept by, and Irem was forever mute!
    A blinding sea of sand
Hid the delight of all the mourning land.

Long ages passed; and men had ceased to heed
  The story, till Colabah sought one day
  A camel which had wandered far away
Beyond Al Ahkaf's dreary plain to feed;
    And as the hour grew late
He found himself within a palace gate.

High, gilded towers within a garden rare,
  A blooming waste from whence all life had flown,
  For vacant windows in the sunlight shone
And fruit, unpluck'd, with sweets oppress'd the air.
    'Mid creamy blossoms hung
Cages of twisted gold that empty swung.

A moment with strange rapture he perceived
   The blaze of beauty, then the deathly calm
Smote him with sudden sense of nameless
     harm.
Backward he turned; yet fain to be believed,
     He grasped with hasty hand
A few, bright pebbles from the sparkling sand.

Then swiftly fleeing, to his comrades bore
   The tale of Irem's splendor lost and found;
   Nor could they scoff, when, from his robe
     unbound,
He showed his treasure of mysterious ore.
     For lo! the sunset kissed
Rare stones of topaz, agate, amethyst!

Vainly at morning's break they searched the
     plain
   For its hid treasure. The unanswering sands
   Kept well the secret of their Genii's hands,
Nor yielded Irem to the world again.
     But with serenest flame
Still glowed the gems and told Colabah's fame.

Ah! thus the Bard whom inspiration leads
   Into the realm of visionary thought.
   In hidden paths, by bowers divinely wrought,

Upon enchanted fruits his fancy feeds.
　　Till suddenly he spies
Unreal splendors deck his Paradise, —

Then fleeing, half in rapture, half in fright,
　He seeks the world of daily life once more;
　The charm is lost, the bloom, the brilliance
　　o'er,
Yet happy if he gathered in his flight,
　　To shine through many days,
One priceless gem of beauty, love or praise.

ST. GREGORY'S GUEST.

At St. Andrew's Convent gate
   Gregory, monk of pious fame,
Day by day at vesper bell
   Heard a beggar call his name.

And from prayer or chanted hymn
   By unwearied patience led,
Still with helpful word and gift
   He the stranger comforted.

All he gave : the relic last,
   Dearest of his meagre store,
Not till then he pitying plead —
   "Importune me, friend, no more !"

Years passed on ; the lowly monk
   Sat upon the pontiff's throne,
The tiara, with the heart
   Of all Rome, was now his own.

Yet in high as low estate
   Gave he richly from his store,

Twelve poor men each eventide
  Supped within his palace door.

And as once he sat with them,
  Earnest each one's need to know,
He perceived a stranger guest
  All the others placed below.

To his steward beckoned he —
  "One unbidden friend is here —
Go, salute him! bid him take
  Freely of our evening cheer."

Down the room the servant passed ; —
  "Only twelve are here to night."
"Count again! behold he sits
  Where the sunshine lingers bright ;

"See his yellow, flowing hair
  Blending with the sunset flame !
Pale his brow, serene his gaze —
  I would know from whence he came."

Once again with troubled haste
  Up and down the steward glides ;
"Twelve good pilgrims sup with thee,
  And no alien 'mid them hides."

" It is well," the Father said,
　　But his heart within him shook;
He perceived that in their midst
　　One unseen the feast partook!

On the room a silence fell,
　　Silence as of heavenly grace —
Ah! how burned the sunset gold
　　On each pilgrim's bended face,

And upon the threshold poised,
　　Mindful of the unwonted spell,
Lo! a silver plumaged dove
　　Trilled a mellow canticle!

One by one the guests withdrew,
　　Then the stranger coming near
Silent paused — the pontiff's lips
　　Trembling asked — " What dost thou here?"

"Gregory! at St. Andrew's gate
　　Oft to me thy alms were given,
Fear not now thy soul's desire
　　In my name to ask of Heaven!"

As he spoke celestial rays
　　Soft around his forehead flowed,

And his form from earth upraised
In a violet nimbus glowed.

Slow the shining vision passed —
All his soul in thanks outpoured,
Blessed Gregory cried aloud,
"I have entertained the Lord!"

A STORM FANTASY.

The lonely wind a Banshee of despair
 Wails through the wintry night,
And the affrighted Moon, no longer fair,
 Veils her wan face from sight.
She knows the signals of that voice and why
With his keen moan he desolates the sky.

The sad, sad Rain comes sobbing at his call,
 She smites the earth with tears —
"There is no rest," she sighs — "no rest in all
 The ever-dying years.
In cloudland hid I would forever stay,
Why call me thence to weep my life away?"

Thus as the ages pass; and who may know
 Or dare to tell again
The legend of these spectres and their woe,
 The grieving Wind and Rain?
Lovers perchance in some primeval world,
For darkest treachery into darkness hurled!

44

Still mocked by hope and haunted by regret
  They seek the earth again,
Yearning to meet each other they forget
  Their wish is always vain.
For he has but a *voice* of wordless woe,
She has but *tears* that blind her as they flow.

O lost, lost spirits of the storm and night!
  Listening to you I know
There is a depth to which no ray of light
  From Heaven's expanse can flow.
Come, Angel of the morning, come again !
Speak "Peace — be still!" unto the Wind and
    Rain.

TÛBA.

'T is written on the flowery page
Of Islam's visionary sage,

That Tûba tree of happiness,
Whose fruit shall all believers bless,

Hath roots whose fibres strong and deep
Beneath the world's foundations sleep,

Yet never wind of earth shall blow
The odors from one spicy bough.

Far up beyond the walls of time
The star-bespangled branches climb,

Up through the musky gardens where
Eternal sunshine gilds the air,

And wingèd Houris flutter by
To low, delicious melody.

There over every palace door
The boughs of Tûba fragrance pour—

46

And sweet bells hung amid the flowers
Ring in and out the joyous hours.

Has not the orient sage declared
A truth which every soul has shared?

We pluck the green leaves of delight —
The branches reach beyond our sight;

The germ of happiness is ours,
But airs diviner hide the flowers.

Here disappointment, gaunt and gray,
Salutes us daily on our way,

The truest love knows direst loss,
The surest triumph bears a cross,

And yet the soul may smile on fate
And with most loyal patience wait,

Believing that on heights unknown
She yet will come unto her own —

Where Islam's tree, transfigured, gleams
With fairer fruit than Islam dreams!

I.

In days of old,
In solitude and silence grew the hour
When God and Nature first beheld unfold
The solitary flower.

Purple as night
Its petals opened in the forest gloom,
And the winds pausing in their seaward flight
Inhaled the strange perfume.

The hoary oak
Felt in its branches a responsive thrill,
The eagle from his lonely eyrie spoke,
And all again was still.

II.

Unwritten ages rolled
Into the past, and as each century's bell
Struck the full hour, the blossom would unfold,
With none its tale to tell.

48

At last the silence ceased,
The desert wilderness a voice had found.
Strange wanderers from the overflowing East
Sought here a hunting ground.

The shadow-haunted glades
Echoed the savage song — the warrior cry —
And wild, barbaric worship filled the shades
With awful mystery.

Life warm and new
Through the dull fibres of the tree was shed;
The swelling buds revealed a living hue —
Tinge of the morning red.

III.

Not unblest
The thousand years of silence and of night;
Unto the hidden gardens of the West
God said — "Let there be light!"

And behold!
It blooms again, the latest flower of Time!
In the dark ages who could have foretold
The glory of its prime?

  Palmiest days
Of Grecian grandeur or of Roman pride
Saw not their century bloom in such a blaze
  Of fame, full-orbed, world-wide.

  Heaven, bend low!
From the last, lingering gloom our land release!
Let the perfection of the ages blow
  White as the plume of Peace!

A TUSCAN LEGEND.

When good St. Ambrose paused at close of day
  Before a Tuscan noble's open door,
With welcome words the host his entrance urged
  And spread before him of his choicest store.

Within, the palace shone with gems of art,
  Bronze, marble, gold, in forms antique and
    rare,
Refreshing fountains tossed a snowy spray,
  And sumptuous roses sweetened all the air.

The fasting saint with thanks the food partook,
  And with his fellow-pilgrims silent shared,
Then, still reclining at the table, sought
  Of his kind host if well or ill he fared.

Glowed with a haughty joy the Tuscan's brow, —
  "All things are well with me," his proud
    reply —
"My wealth provides for each luxurious want,
  Nor knows ambition one unanswered sigh.

51

"My slaves, obedient, watch my lightest look;
  My children, beautiful, enhance my joy;
Pain, mourning, in this palace are unknown,
  My state is happiness without alloy."

What said the saint? Up from that lordly
      board
  He rose in haste, his visage pale with fear,
    And to the startled pilgrims cried aloud,
  "Flee from this place! the Lord abides not
      here."

Outspoken saint! Thy words may well convey
  Terror and comfort to the end of time;
Woe, to the soul sufficient to itself,
  But to the stricken, prophecy sublime.

Grief is the shadow of the Lord's approach,
  Darkness, the pathway of the Bethlehem
      star, —
Let him exult whom sacred sorrow leads
  To reach for God, and find He is not far!

THE HELIOTROPE.

SOMEWHERE 't is told that in an Eastern land,
Clasped in the dull palm of a mummy's hand
A few light seeds were found : with wondering
        eyes
And words of awe was lifted up the prize.

And much they marvelled what could be so
        dear
Of herb or flower as to be treasured here,
What sacred vow had made the dying keep
So close this token for his last long sleep.

None ever knew, but in the fresh, warm earth
The cherished seeds sprang to a second birth,
And eloquent once more with love and hope
Burst into bloom the purple heliotrope.

Embalmed, perhaps, with sorrow's fiery tears,
Out of the silence of a thousand years
It answered back the passion of the past
With the pure breath of perfect peace at last.

53

O pulseless heart! as ages pass, sleep well!
The purple flower thy secret will not tell,
But only to our eager quest reply,
"Love, hidden in the grave, can never die."

THE FIRST AT THE FEAST.

St. Martin once, an honored guest,
    Sat at the royal board ;
With his own hand a cup of wine
    The gracious sovereign poured,
And bade, with smiles, the favored priest
Drink first, as greatest at the feast.

The father took the sparkling cup, —
    With priceless gems it blazed, —
And down the gleaming banquet hall
    In thoughtful silence gazed.
How shone the place with splendors rare!
Was he indeed the greatest there?

What to the King of Kings availed
    This pomp of earthly state?
What unto Him were crown and throne
    And soldiers at the gate ?
The flowers, the lights, the lustrous gold,
The music that voluptuous rolled?

55

Would Heaven's high Sovereign deem him great,
   Because a fleeting hour
He sunned himself in royal smiles
   And shared imperial power?
Ah! nobler far the humblest there
Who meekly served in trust and prayer.

"Not unto me!" he spoke at last—
   And beckoned with his hand
To a poor priest who waiting stood
   To hear his least command.
" By worldly glory undefiled,
Drink thou, our Master's worthier child!"

The priest obeyed; the monarch heard
   A voice beyond his own;
Nobles and warriors bowed in awe
   Of a superior throne.
And in the hush St. Martin's face
Seemed to illumine all the place!

TEARS OF ISIS.

When Isis, by true mother love oppressed,
Held wounded Horus to her goddess breast,
Each tear that touched the sympathetic earth
To some rich, aromatic herb gave birth.

Such healing sprang from her celestial pain,
Mortals no longer seek relief in vain,
For oft as spring awakes the slumbering years,
In wood and meadow blossom Isis' tears.

O Goddess of the starry lotus bloom!
Thou didst foreshadow many a lonely doom;
Thy sorrow by divinest alchemy
Could comfort others, — who could comfort
    thee?

57

VIDAR THE SILENT.

WHEN the last bird flutters southward
  As the sunlight fainter glows,
And into the dim November
  A pensive stillness flows,
When the mountain summits wrap them
  In robes of brown and gold,
I think of the Norsemen's Vidar,
  The silent god of old.

He dwells in the boundless forests,
  In pathless wilds unknown,
He loves the breeze-rocked prairies,
  And the mountains are his own.
In the bloom of songful summer
  He shuns the haunts of men,
But he comes with the days of darkness
  To look on the world again.

By the bleak and desolate sea-shore
  The waves their tumult cease,
The rivulets know his footfall
  And tremble into peace.

The wind steals into the forest,
   The tall trees watchful stand,
And the stars hang mute and pensive
As he roams the leafless land.

.

No voice nor speech has Vidar,
   And his features no man knows,
But he lays his hand ou the heart-strings
   And wonderful music flows;
As if the reverberations
   Of a long and sorrowful past
Were slowly ascending and blending
   With the peace that shall come at last.

Thus Vidar the Silent passes
   Over the world's wide space,
Giving to all who greet him
   One beautiful hour of grace.
Then welcome the tuneless branches!
   Welcome the darkened days!
There shall be light on the shadows
   And in the stillness, praise.

SONG OF PLYMOUTH ROCK.

A THOUSAND years I kept
My watch by the slumbering sea,
A thousand omens read
Of the day that was coming to me.

'T was uttered by wind and wave
And whispered by cloud and star,
" The soul of Freedom sleeps until
The ' Mayflower ' sails from far."

The tide came surging up
From the depths of ocean's caves,
And ever a promise brought
Of the bark that would cross the waves,

The tide went rolling down
In surf and swell and foam,
And ever I dreamed it ran to bid
The " Mayflower " welcome home!

It fell with the falling snow,
The word of fate at last,

And the hailing bell of freedom rang
  In the stormy, wintry blast.

"O sea!" I said — "be kind!
  Be faithful sky and star!
With priceless freight to all the land
  The "Mayflower" rides afar.

She was moored within the bay,
  Pale blossom of the sea —
And the boats went to and fro
  Until all were brought to me.

O I had waited long
  For the touch of those pilgrim feet:
The wintry air grew redolent
  With incense strange and sweet,

For the gate of heaven swung wide
  And angels thronged the air,
As that Pilgrim band their voices raised
  In fervent praise and prayer.

They were feeble, faint and few,
  That little sea-tossed flock,
But never on earth will the echo die,
  Of that prayer upon the Rock.

The wanderers passed on
    To watch and toil and die,
And the "Mayflower" homeward sailed
    And was lost in the morning sky;

But wide over all the land,
    Free as the sunlight's ray,
Grow the fearless faith, the fervent zeal
    Which came to shore that day.

Now evermore I watch
    By the side of the sounding sea,
Muse and ponder and dream
    Of the glory that came to me.

For Freedom crossed the deep
    To a heritage unknown;
The "Mayflower" was her ark of hope,
    The Rock her altar-stone.

NOROMBEGA.

MIDSUMMER'S crimson moon
Above the hills like some night-opening rose
Uplifted, pours its beauty down the vale
    Where broad Penobscot flows.

The night is all in bloom
With subtle sweetness from the skies distilled,
The vesper wind in whispers steals along,
    By the soft silence thrilled.

Of old the fairy world
Held royal revel on midsummer's eve,
Once more along the moonbeams they may come
    The twinkling dance to weave;

Or by the moonlight spell
Entranced, and listening with attentive ear,
The drowsy whispers of the ripening leaves
    And harvests, I may hear.

Now on the field of night
No longer blooms one solitary rose!

With countless groups of silver-petalled stars
    The infinite garden glows,

    And the transfigured moon,
Grown paler, clearer, like a lily white,
Immaculate in beauty, hangs above
    The starry wreath of night.

    A splendid glamour drowns
All sound in silence; even the lapping wave
Just trembles to the shore, with stilly touch
    The lonely rock to lave.

    And I remember now,
That this is haunted ground.   In ages past
Here stood the storied Norombega's walls
    Magnificent and vast.

    The streets were ivory-paved,
The stately walls were built of golden ore,
Its domes outshone the sunset, and full boughs
    Hesperian fruitage bore.

    And up this winding flood
Has wandered many a sea-tossed, daring bark,
While eager eyes have scanned the rugged shore,
    Or pierced the wildwood dark ;

But watched in vain : afar
They saw the spires gleam golden on the sky,
The distant drum-beat heard, or bugle note,
    Wound wildly, fitfully —

    Banners of strange device
Beckoned from distant heights, yet as the stream
Narrowed among the hills, the city fled,
    A mystery, or a dream.

    In the deep forest hid
Like the enchanted princess of romance,
Wooing an endless search, yet still secure
    In her unbroken trance.

    O city of the Past !
No mirage of the wilderness wert thou !
Though yet unfreed from the mysterious spell,
    I deem thee slumbering now.

    Perhaps invisible feet
White-sandalled pass amid the moonbeams pale,
Yon shadow-wave may be some lordly barge
    Drifting with phantom sail.

    The legend was not all
A myth, it was a prophecy as well :

In Norombega's cloud-wrapt palaces
  The living yet shall dwell.

  Fed by its hundred lakes
Here shall the river run o'er golden sands,
These hills in burnished tower and temple shine
  Beneath the builder's hands !

  Where tarries still the hour
When the true knight shall the enchantment
    break,
Unveil the peerless city of the east,
  The charmèd princess wake ?

  Till then, O River, tell
To none but dreaming bards the Future's boon !
Till then guard thou the mystery of the vale,
  Midsummer midnight moon !

KINEO.

How beautiful the morning breaks
Upon the King of mountain lakes!
The forests, far as eye can reach,
Stretch green and still from either beach,
And leagues away the water's gleam
Resplendent in the sunrise beam;
Yet feathery vapors, circling slow
Wreathe the dark brow of Kineo.

The hermit Mount in sullen scorn
Repels the rosy touch of morn,
As some remorseful, lonely heart,
From human pleasure set apart,
Shrinks even from the tender touch
Of pity, lest it yield too much,
So speechless still to friend or foe,
Frowns the black cliff of Kineo.

Yet, as the whispering ripples break
From the still surface of the lake
On the repellent rocks, they seem
To murmur low, as in a dream,

The mountain's name, and day by day
The listening breezes bear away
A memory of the long ago.,
A sad, wild tale of Kineo.

How many moons can no man say
O'er heaven's blue sea have sailed away,
Since Kineo and his fleet canoe
First vanished from his kindred's view.
Hunter and warrior, lithe and keen,
No brave on all the lake was seen
Whose wigwam could such trophies show,
As the green roof of Kineo.

But wrathful, jealous, quick to strife,
He lived a passion-darkened life;
Even Maquaso, his mother, fled
His baneful lodge in mortal dread.
Then gathering round the midnight fire,
The old men spake with threatenings dire
"Out from our councils he must go,
The demon-haunted Kineo!"

In sullen and remorseful mood
He gave himself to solitude.
Up the wild rocks by night he bore
Of all he prized a stealthy·store, —

Flint, arrows, knife and birch. Who knows
But some dark lock or dead wild rose,
The phantom of an untold woe,
Shared the lone haunt of Kineo?

The mountain was his own ; than he
None other dared its mystery.
None sought to meet the savage glare
Of the wild hunter in his lair :
But when far up the mountain side
Each night a lurid flame they spied,
The watchful red men muttered low,
"There hides our brother Kineo."

Years passed. Among the storm-swept pines
From moon to moon he read the signs
Of blossom and decay. He knew
The eagle that familiar flew
About his path. The fearless bird
His melancholy accents heard,
But glen or shore no more might know
The swift, still step of Kineo,

Save once. His tribe in deadly fray
Had battled all the lowering day,
And many a brave Penobscot's blood
Was mingling in the lake's pure flood,

When like a spectre, through the gloom,
With gleaming knife and eagle plume,
And glance that burned with lurid glow,
Strode the bold form of Kineo!

A hush like death — and then a cry,
Fierce and exultant, pierced the sky!
They rallied round that fiery plume
And smote the foe with hopeless doom.
But when the grateful warriors fain
Would seek his well-known face again,
Their gifts and homage to bestow,
Gone, like a mist, was Kineo.

They saw him not, but from that hour
They bowed before his wizard power;
His watch-fire grew to be a shrine
Half terrible and half divine.
None ever knew when death drew nigh,
When into darker mystery
Of cloud above or deep below
Stole the sad ghost of Kineo.

But when his camp-fire burned no more,
The solitary mountain bore
His name; and when at times the sky
Grew dark, a long, despairing sigh

Down the dark precipices rolled
And tempest terrible foretold.
The fishers feared the wind, the snow,
The lightning, less than Kineo.

Now beautiful the morning skies
Look on this forest paradise;
Fresh voices, loud and joyous, wake
The echoes of the grand old lake:
But underneath that frowning height
The shadow and the spell of night
Come back: the oars fall still and slow,
The waves sigh, *Peace to Kineo!*

THE BOWDOIN OAK.

Planted in 1802 by George Thorndike, a member of the
first class of Bowdoin. He died at the age of twenty-one,
the only one of that class remembered by the students of
Bowdoin to-day. — *Oration of T. R. Simonton.*

YE breezy boughs of Bowdoin's oak,
  Sing low your summer rune!
In murmuring, rhythmic tones respond
  To every breath of June;

And memories of the joyous youth,
  Through all your songs repeat,
Who plucked the acorn from the twig
  Blown lightly to his feet,

And gayly to his fellows cried:
  "My destiny behold!
This seed shall keep my memory green
  In ages yet untold.

"I trust it to the sheltering sod,
  I hail the promised tree!
Sing, unborn oak, through long decades,
  And ever sing of me!"

By cloud and sunbeam nourished well,
   The tender sapling grew,
Less stalwart than the rose which drank
   From the same cup of dew;

But royal blood was in its veins,
   Of true Hellenic line,
And sunward reached its longing arms
   With impulses divine.

The rushing river as it passed
   Caught whispers from the tree,
And each returning tide brought back
   The answer of the sea.

Till to the listening groves a voice,
   New and harmonious, spoke,
And from a throne of foliage looked
   The spirit of the oak!

Then birds of happiest omen built
   High in its denser shade,
And grand responses to the storms
   The sounding branches made.

Beneath its bower the bard beloved
   His budding chaplet wore,

The wizard king of romance dreamed
His wild, enchanting lore;

And scholars, musing in its shade,
Here heard their country's cry —
Their lips gave back — " O sweet it is
For native land to die! "

With hearts that burned they cast aside
These peaceful, oaken bays;
The hero's blood-red path they trod —
Be theirs the hero's praise.

Oh, though Dodona's voice is hushed,
A new, intenser flame
Stirs the proud oak to whisper still
Some dear illustrious name!

And what of him whose happy mood
Foretold this sylvan birth?
In boyhood's prime he sank to rest;
His work was done on earth.

Brief was his race, and light his task
For immortality,
His only tribute to the years
The planting of a tree.

Sing low, green oak, thy summer rune,
  Sing valor, love and truth,
Thyself a fair, embodied thought,
  A living dream of youth.

LYRICS.

77

LYRICS.

EASTER MORNING.

I.

Ostera ! spirit of springtime,
  Awake from thy slumbers deep!
Arise! and with hands that are glowing,
  Put off the white garments of sleep!
Make thyself fair, O goddess!
  In new and resplendent array,
For the footsteps of Him who has risen
  Shall be heard in the dawn of day.

Flushes the trailing arbutus
  Low under the forest leaves, —
A sign that the drowsy goddess
  The breath of her Lord perceives.

79

While He suffered, her pulse beat numbly;
  While He slept, she was still with pain;
But now He awakes — He has risen —
  Her beauty shall bloom again.

O hark! in the budding woodlands,
  Now far, now near, is heard
The first prelusive warble
  Of rivulet and of bird.
O listen! the Jubilate
  From every bough is poured,
And earth in the smile of the springtime
  Arises to greet her Lord!

II.

Radiant goddess Aurora!
  Open the chambers of dawn;
Let the Hours like a garland of graces
  Encircle the chariot of morn.
Thou dost herald no longer Apollo,
  The god of the sunbeam and lyre;
The pride of his empire is ended,
  And pale is his armor of fire.

From a loftier height than Olympus
  Light flows, — from the Temple above, —

And the mists of old legends are scattered
  In the dawn of the Kingdom of Love.
Come forth from the cloudland of fable,
  For day in full splendor make room,
For a triumph that lost not its glory
  As it paused in the sepulchre's gloom.

She comes! the bright goddess of morning,
  In crimson and purple array,
Far down on the hill-tops she tosses
  The first golden lilies of day.
O'er the mountains her sandals are glowing,
  O'er the valleys she speeds on the wing,
Till earth is all rosy and radiant
  For the feet of the new-risen King.

III.

Open the gates of the Temple;
  Spread branches of palm and of bay;
Let not the spirits of Nature
  Alone deck the Conqueror's way.
While Spring from her death-sleep arises,
  And joyous His presence awaits,
While Morning's smile lights up the Heavens,
  Open the Beautiful Gates!

He is here! the long watches are over,
　　The stone from the grave rolled away;
" We shall sleep," was the sigh of the midnight·
　　" We shall rise," is the song of to-day.
O Music! no longer lamenting,
　　On pinions of tremulous flame
Go soaring to meet the Beloved,
　　And swell the new song of His fame!

The altar is snowy with blossoms,
　　The font is a vase of perfume,
On pillar and chancel are twining
　　Fresh garlands of eloquent bloom.
Christ is risen! with glad lips we utter;
　　And far up the infinite height
Archangels the pæan re-echo,
　　And crown Him with lilies of Light!

URANIA.

From what superior star
Gazing, entranced, afar,
Didst thou first look on earth when earth was
young?
Thou whom the singers of all days have sung,
Spirit of Song! by many names adored,
Whose deep, sweet speech, the music of the
soul,
Our human utterance cannot yet control,
Upon whose dazzling shrine are ceaseless offer-
ings poured.

When first thy sun-shod feet
Pressed the new verdure, sweet
With timid violet and virgin rose,
When first thy rainbow plumage passing by,
The shepherd bards discerned, ah ! rapturously
They sought thy inspiration to disclose.
With burning heart and glances raised above,
Speech overflowed in song, and all their theme
was love.

Nor didst thou linger long
In vales of pastoral song.
Judea's harp thy fervid fingers strung.
The groves of palm, the sacred rivers heard,
The cedars upon Lebanon were stirred
When David's lips immortal measures sung.
And smoke of costliest odors rose to heaven
With chorus and response by Hebrew voices
  given.

On Orpheus' glowing lyre
Was laid thy touch of fire;
By thy own lips, on Sappho's brow was pressed
The mystic kiss which woke her soul's unrest.
Unveiled by thee in thy most radiant mood
The palaces that on Olympus stood,
From whose charmed portals came at thy
  decree
The gods of earth and heaven, the nymphs of
  air and sea.

Then was the age of gold,
When bards heroic told
Heroic legends of primeval days.
Then had the singer his full meed of praise,
For thou didst touch the laurel with thy wand,
And prince and warrior with exultant hand

Wove the bright bays around the minstrel's
name.
Their valor was his theme; his song their surest
fame.

Yet not by these was seen
The splendor of thy mien,
The full, unclouded glory of thy face;
These caught but glimpses of the light divine,
And counting thee among the "sacred nine,"
Groped in the darkness for thy dwelling-place.
Milton alone o'er elder bards prevailed,
Upon the starry heights he saw thy brow unveiled.

Dearer through ages grown,
Thou wilt not leave alone
The world thy presence has made half divine.
Still countless votaries bow before thy shrine;
The Norseman's ringing ballad, the soft chime
Of Spanish lute to silver-sandalled rhyme,
The hymn of freedom by the sunset sea,
Or Persia's passion-lays, all sacred are to thee.

Some are content to reach
The still, inaudible speech
Of winds and woods and waters' rhythmic flow;
These know thee best in Nature's whispers low,

And with the hem of thy rich garment pressed
To tuneful lips, they are supremely blest.
Others have caught a more transcendent gleam,
And greet thee on the heights of prophecy and
    dream.

Stay, thou resplendent one!
Not yet thy task is done, —
Not yet the perfect song of ages sung!
A rose unblown it sleeps upon thy breast,
Waiting to make some later Eden blest.
Still be the halo of thy beauty flung
Over dark days, dark years, until afar
Above the new song's birth, thou smilest like a
    a star!

ONLY WAITING.

Only waiting till the shadows
    Are a little longer grown,
Only waiting till the glimmer
    Of the day's last beam is flown;
Till the night of earth is faded
    From this heart once full of day,
Till the dawn of Heaven is breaking
    Through the twilight soft and gray.

Only waiting till the reapers
    Have the last sheaf gathered home,
For the summer-time hath faded
    And the autumn winds are come.
Quickly, reapers, gather quickly
    The last ripe hours of my heart —
For the bloom of life is withered,
    And I hasten to depart.

Only waiting till the angels
    Open wide the mystic gate,
At whose feet I long have lingered,
    Weary, poor, and desolate.

Even now I hear their footsteps
  And their voices far away:
If they call me I am waiting, —
  Only waiting to obey.

Only waiting till the shadows
  Are a little longer grown,
Only waiting till the glimmer
  Of the day's last beam is flown;
Then from out the folded darkness
  Holy, deathless stars shall rise,
By whose light my soul will gladly
  Wing her passage to the skies.

ARCADIA.

WE heard it first on an April morn,
  If rung by fairies I cannot tell,
But earth was smiling o'er flowers new-born,
  And birds home coming to wood and dell
With jubilant music saluted the dawn,
    When far in the distance we heard a sweet
      bell, —
A flute-like echo, a dulcet strain,
That pierced our hearts with a tender pain, —
    The bell-call of Arcadia.

" Where can we find it?" we asked the wise
  Who musing sat in the willow shade.
They, looking on us with wistful eyes,
  Answer vague to our question made:
" Nor east nor west that fair land lies, —
  A seal of magic is on it laid ;
But love and longing the spell unbind,
And he who follows at last may find
    The hidden land, Arcadia.

"Down evergreen mountains in sparkling sheen
    A hundred rivulets seek the sea;
Flocks, snow-white, feed in the pastures green,
    And under the boughs of the dark fir-tree
To shepherd minstrels of joyous mien
    The wood-god Pan pipes cheerily.
Always summer days, blithe and long.
Always melody, bloom, and song,
        In the fair land of Arcadia."

We could not linger.   With hearts that beat
    Wild with longing and fond desire,
We followed the call of the bell so sweet.
    "Soon," we said, "will that sylvan lyre
With witching welcome our senses greet.
    Ere sunset brightens yon purple spire
We shall rest among roses our weary feet."
    Was it fancy?   The dear home violets' eyes
Seemed brimming with tears of sad surprise —
        But away to rare Arcadia!

Many a morning's ruddy tide
    Flooded the midnight's desolate bar,
Many a sunset splendor died, —
    Yet Hope rekindled the evening star,
And still o'er desert or mountain side
    We heard the silvery chime afar,

Calling " Hither, O pilgrim feet,
Here your rest shall be full and sweet
   In green groves of Arcadia."

At times the kiss of a sudden breeze
   With tropic odors our senses stirred,
Breath of scarlet pomegranite trees
   And lotus blossoms. We surely heard
The low, soft rhythm of summer seas,
   The brooding note of the Halcyon bird.
Onward we pressed : so near, at last,
One more brief shadow of woodland past,
   And then — our blest Arcadia!

But after the woodland, the black ravine,
   And further, a long, lone mountain height,
There, as we clambered with saddened mien,
   In the fading Autumn's sunset light —
For the leaves were russet that once were
     green —
Pilgrims numberless met our sight,
Snow-white locks on the evening wind,
   And mournfully, steadfastly looking behind
    They sighed, " Farewell, Arcadia ! "

We too looked back, and a wonderful light
   Lay on the landscape our feet had passed ;

Clearer the morning and softer than night,
  O'er all the road was the glamor cast.
And there, revealed to our yearning sight,
  The beautiful valley lay at last.
Far back where the April violets grew,
There smiled, amid crystals of deathless dew,
  Our first and last Arcadia !

A BUDDHIST VISION.

I.

In his night-watch beneath the Banian tree
  Buddha, the blessed, saw the years unsealed,
And change on change of wondrous destiny
  In his own life revealed ;

Saw the long path of darkness and of pain,
  From tiger crouching in his jungle lair,
To priest grown wan with fasting and with
    prayer
      Nirvana's peace to gain..

If for one hour his vision we might share,
  His moonlight faith accepting, stand aside
From the strong sunshine of to-day, and dare
    Down the dark past to glide,

By what fantastic labyrinths of space,
  Through what ripe moments of unconscious
    doom,
What endless links of motion, music, bloom,
    Our lineage we might trace!

II.

My eyes were opened. Down the years unknown,
  In a dim forest I beheld afar
  A fragile plant amid whose leaves had grown
    One blossom, like a star.

Nurtured in gloom, in speechless solitude
  It watched the hour which brought a sunbeam
      near,
Thus opening, fading, many a hopeless year,
    Till strange unrest imbued

Its feeble pulse. Unheard of all its kind
  Its first, last sigh was breathed. And lo! no
      more·
A blossom, but a lightly wandering wind
      It roamed the woodland o'er!

Out where the sunshine gilded all the land
  It tossed the long plumes of the ripening
      wheat,
  Or seaward ran, the joyous waves to meet,
And played along the strand,

How long I know not. In a greenwood nook
  It found a rivulet dancing in the sun,

It lingered, dallied, whispered with the brook
    Till wave and wind were one.

O then what joy in melody new-born!
    What dimpled, prattling infancy of song,
    In summer twilights beautiful and long,
        And in the rosy dawn!

Until green branches waving free and strong
    Mingled above the stream in choral high;
The brook was hushed, — it heard a nobler song
        And nearer to the sky.

So when the summer burned along the lea,
    And fiery drought crept down the withered glen,
    The spirit of the brook went forth again
        Into a laurel tree.

Now was it conscious of a larger life,
    Wide outlook, vigorous growth, the welcome
        change
Of freshening foliage. Every pulse was rife
        With strivings new and strange.

Exultant in its beauty, ardent beams
    Swelled the rich buds and burst the creamy
        flowers,

Yet as it rocked the birds in tuneful hours
It heard, as if in dreams,

A note its solemn measure had not learned,
A tone all other melodies above
Of wind, or wave or boughs that skyward turned,—
It was the note of love!

Stricken at last the tree gave forth its breath, —
Far in a tropic nest a birdling stirred.
O nightingale! no passing wing of death
Thy waking rapture heard.

Cradled in roses, upon roses fed,
Sweeter, diviner grew thy honeyed strain,
The tender, haunting, passionate refrain
Of many summers fled.

Unto a state of royalty was risen
The spirit which forever had desired
A height untried, and like a soul in prison
Still panted and aspired.

There came a sun-winged seraph. Stooping low
He whispered, " Singer, yet another change
Must come. Thy song, to reach sublimest range,
Must human sorrow know."

And thus it came to pass one starry dawn
  The nightingale would never waken more;
But in the northland by a stormy shore
    A poet-child was born, —

With many gifts and riches for his dower,
  The deep desire for beauty and for light
Which rent the pale soul of the forest flower,
    And the intense delight

In freedom which the roving wind had known, —
  Such rapture as had thrilled the brook, the
    tree,
With love beyond the bulbul's minstrelsy,
    And sorrow's mightier tone.

III.

Return, O Vision! Shed one other ray
  If from Nirvana or the holier Heaven!
The years fall fast, — the Poet must away:
    What new song shall be given?

The veil is dropt. Gautama's blissful shade
  Is vanished and the brief illusion fled.
I only know that every life must fade,
    And silent are the dead.

But if from many and from fair estates
   Comes the true accent to the Poet's lips,
   Rich heritage beyond this last eclipse
      The high-born Singer waits.

GREENWOOD GREETINGS.

THE morning of the year
Flushes again these northern glades. Awake,
O slumbering branches ! Once again the cheer
And comradeship of other summers take
On your mute faces. Answer me again,
And tell your winter's dream of ecstasy or pain.

Then first the maples stirred,
Their drooping blossoms trembling with delight,
And said — "The night is over ! we have heard
The brook rejoicing in the breaking light —
The rapture of the rain
Over the lost arbutus, found again ;
The sod grows velvet green beneath our feet ;
Homeward the robins fly, and life again is
sweet !"

The pine tree flung
Its tassels to the wind and proudly sung, —
"I dreamed of lands where over leagues of ice
The skaters joyous flew. Of northern lights

99

Flaming along the skies in strange device,
Of reindeer speeding through the glimmering
   nights.
The forest trembled with old Odin's signs
Of stormy pain, but all undaunted sung the
   pines!"

     The elm returned —
"Of summer was my dream the long night
   through,
Of sunset-fires where myriad roses burned,
Giving their beauty back in morning dew.
     Of interlacing boughs
Festooned in arches meet for lover's vows,
And of the golden robin's nest that clung
Near to my heart, which throbbed whene'er the
   birdlings sung."

     Rough-hooded fir,
Why dost thou beckon to the juniper
With signs of joy? Slow waved her rustling fan
As she replied: "I heard in my long dream
The mellow pipe, far blown, of jocund Pan
Invisible by wood and valley stream.
He is not dead, the god of dell and grove,
But with him, joyous still, the nymphs and
   satyrs rove!"

The poplar trees
Their odorous buds all quivering in the
    breeze,
Sighed — "Heavy was our sleep and dark
    with gloom
The dreaded vision of the night.   Of yore
The fated poplar grew unto its doom
And powerless fell. Shaped from its shuddering
    wood
The Cross was fashioned.   Now and evermore
That woe returns.   The stain of holy blood
        Our slumber haunts alway,
And every waking leaf still trembles with
    dismay."

        The willow's plume
Swept the warm sod with downy tufts of
    bloom.
" O willow ! thou dost ever earthward gaze
And sighs are all thy language."   And the
    tree
Whispered — " I feel again the flowery days
Of a new year, but spring the fair, the free,
Cannot bring back the beautiful to me.
There is sound of tear-drops in the rain,
Of mourning in the air.   The lost come not
    again."

Ah! then the cedars bent
Their glossy crowns and spake with deep
content:
" We have not slept nor dreamed the livelong
night!
In our dark mantles wrapped we watched
for light.
We are the faithful.   In our spicy boughs
The breath of Lebanon forever flows.
Summer or winter, life or death may be,
Hope gathers garlands green from off the cedar
tree! "

O kindred of the wood,
Lift up your heads! for now the sunrise beams
Scatter the mist of darkness and of dreams:
The world is made anew and it is good!
A thousand voices herald summer's day, —
Let us drink deep from life's fresh fountains
while we may.

THE FIRST ROBIN.

Welcome again, from the land of the summer,
  Bird in the maple with jubilant song!
Nodding and singing thy rapturous greeting,
  Where hast thou stayed from our garden
    so long?
Often the little ones looked from the window,
  When the soft snowflakes fell fleecy and
    dumb,
Saying, "See, mother! the white bees are
    swarming;
  When will they go and the red robins come?"

Rocked on the bough of the silver-leafed maple,
  Hast thou one sigh for the orange and palm?
Could the magnolia's sweet-scented blossoms
  Waft o'er thy sleep a more exquisite balm?
Bird of the North! thou hast winged thy way
    homeward,
  Led by a love that was constant and strong,
On the same bough that in other days rocked
    thee,
  Build a new nest, but, oh! sing the old song

103

Herald art thou of the pageant approaching,
　The floral procession of Summer our queen!
Let the winds harken, and hasten the sunbeams
　To spread for her chariot a carpet of green.
Bid the trees hang out their banners of welcome,
　Red and white banners of beautiful bloom ;
Sing, happy bird, till thy comrades advancing
　Shall rout the last spectre of winter and
　　gloom.

VIOLETS.

I know a spot where woods are green,
  And all the dim, delicious June
A brook flows fast the boughs between
  And trills an eager, joyous tune.
  In clear unbroken melody
  The brook sings and the birds reply :
    " The violets — the violets ! "

Upon the water's velvet edge
  The purple blossoms breathe delight,
Close nestled to the grassy sedge
  As sweet as dawn, as dark as night.
  O brook and branches, far away,
  My heart keeps time with you to-day !
    " The violets — the violets ! "

I sometimes dream that when at last
  My life is done with fading things,
Again will blossom forth the past
  To which my memory fondest clings.
  That some fair star has kept for me,
  Fresh blooming still by brook and tree,
    " The violets — the violets ! "

THE FEAST OF THE VALLEY.

In elder days, beside the tawny Nile
  Where royally embalmed the Pharaohs slept,
Year after year with pomp of flags and flowers
  A beautiful and sacred feast was kept.

Feast of the valley: when the living bore
  Tribute of fruits and incense to the dead,
Marching in gay procession, richly robed,
  By the proud voice of drum and trumpet led.

And nothing doubted they that souls beloved,
  Sailing the blue skies in Osiris' car,
Perceived in slumberous calm the fragrant gifts,
  And heard the music, as in dreams, afar.

Thus in the garb of triumph we would keep
  Memorial Day, the New World's feast of
    flowers;
What shadow can the silent valley hold,
  Since glorified by such a faith as ours!

166

With banners beautiful and songs that tell
  The pride and promise of sweet Freedom's
      home,
Where sleep the sons who loved her unto death,
  With garlands and with trophies we will
      come.

Fair was the grave beneath the Orient palms,
  While Heaven was dumb and yet unsealed the
      tomb,
For us the heavy stone is rolled away, —
  The valley shows a light beyond the gloom.

And from their white encampments on the hills
  Beyond our vision, the beloved reply —
" Here Freedom smiles in a diviner air,
  And, oh, 'tis sweet for native land to die ! "

PEARLS OF PRICE.

LIFE, I fain would ask of thee
Gifts that shall abide with me!
When the tinsel and the dross
Fall away in utter loss —
When my spirit trembling stands
Just within the border lands,
All that I have called my own
Fading in that light unknown,
Let me not with desolate heart
See familiar joys depart.
    Thou art rich, O Life, and I
    For thy choicest guerdon sigh.
    Give me things that cannot die!

Now while days are long and sweet
In midsummer, — while my feet
Falter not amid the bloom,
And no warning signs of doom
In the earth or sky foretell
Swift departure, long farewell,
Let me turn with strength divine
From this bright, bewildering wine,

Life's illusion, — and perceive
What at nightfall I must leave.
 Though it be through dearth and dole
 I would follow to the goal
 Treasure deathless as the soul.

Wide and loving brotherhood
With the gifted and the good,
Fellowship and joy intense
In glad nature's opulence;
Heart of calm and steadfast cheer,
Friendship deepening year by year,
Love that does not fear to wait
For its answer at Heaven's gate,
Faith, a beacon full in sight,
Cloud by day and flame by night, —
 These are riches, treasure, power,
 Which outlive the fatal hour;
 Buds of time which Heaven will flower.

Surely down the sunset road
Comes the messenger of God,
Withering in his glance of fire
Every fleeting, vain desire.
At his touch will melt away
Fairest idols made of clay,

And in hopeless dust fall down
Robe and wreath and rosy crown.
Life, I will not let thee go
Till thy utmost boon I know!
Let my soul's one triumph be,
Ere we part, to win from thee
Jewels for eternity!

THE SIGNAL.

From yonder dormer window
  For many a year has shone
A lamp whose nightly message
  Was borne to me alone;
For there a saintly lady
  Watched for my answering light,
And to my little ones and me
  Wafted her sweet " Good-night."

How often when the evening
  Shut down on days of care,
When heart and brain were heavy
  With burdens hard to bear,
That beam of tranquil brightness
  Her holier calm expressed,
And to my troubled spirit spoke
  Of patience and of rest.

To-night I sit in sadness
  To sing my cradle hymn,
The window is all darkened,
  The house is bleak and dim;

111

Across the fields of moonlight
  No glittering ray is shed,
The lamp is out, the chamber dark,
  The saintly lady dead.

But just above the gable
  With splendid beam afar,
And with unwonted beauty
  Hangs low the evening star!
Is that to be my signal
  As years again go by?
Am I to lift my eyes and read
  Love's language in the sky?

I take the happy omen,
  The lovelight from afar;
The watcher is exalted,
  The lamp is now a star!
Still shall I read the message
  In golden letters clear —
Still to my little ones and me
  The signal is " good cheer ! "

A DREAMLAND CITY.

SOMETIMES the guarded gates
Of the unseen on outward hinges roll,
And in deep dreams of night the troubled
    soul
In bright, brief vision sees the glory of its goal.

Some angel, watchful, kind,
Stoops for the moment from his kindred band,
Reaches, through veil of sleep, a pitying hand,
And leads the Dreamer forth into a fairer land.

Such boon to me was given,
Thus to my sorrow came a sweet release ;
Sleep's magic touches gave to pain surcease ;
And forth my spirit passed into transcendent
    peace.

A city beautiful
Shone on my vision. Palaces of white
And gleaming marble, in a noonday light
Glittered along wide streets with pearly pave-
    ments bright.

Amaranth and asphodel
Above each pillared door their blossoms
    hung;
From every mansion mystic music rung,
For Poesie was here the only voice and tongue.

High in the city's midst
Arose a Temple, as the sunset bright;
Of flame-like splendor, dazzling to the
    sight, —
Arch, column, altar glowed with an interior light.

" This is the shrine of song,"
A voice beside me uttered.   " This her home,
Her chosen dwelling. Hither none may
    come
But her beloved, her own.   Fame's worshippers
    are dumb

" Forth from her temple flows
Perpetual inspiration.   Glorious themes
Break on the vision in ecstatic gleams.
Embodied here the bard beholds his rarest
    dreams.

" Hither the minstrels throng —
The masters wearing laurels centuries old,

Bards who the harp-strings smote with fingers
  bold,
And they whose softer lays with faltering lips
  were told.

  "Nor they alone whose brows
  On earth the victor's sparkling wreath have
    worn,
  These, too whom Fate of every bliss hath
    shorn,
Save of the matchless boon — that they were
  singers born."

  Even as he spoke there rolled
  From out that inner shrine a tide of song.
  Each outer voice the anthem bore along ;
The angel at my side responded full and strong.

  "This is, indeed, my home ! "
I cried. "Here every grief I may forget ;
  Here even for me are peace and rapture met."
My guide, in tender voice replied, " Not yet."

  The dream was at an end.
  Yet in its light I walked through many days,
  Seeing no darkness in them, for my gaze
Illumined once, still burned with the celestial rays.

Now singing as I go,
Little I heed although the path is long;
Light from above hath made my spirit
    strong, —
It is enough to be the humblest child of Song.

And I will be content
To love her for herself; with homage sweet
To sing unheard, unanswered at her feet,
Till in some other life I make my song complete.

RECOMPENSE.

GRIEVE not, beloved, that in such narrow space
Your hopes must still their sparkling plumage
    hide,
Brooding unseen : while others sing and soar,
That you alone go in and out no more.
Write on the threshold of this prison place —
    Eternity is wide!

Sigh not that years unanswering pass away,
And life seems all a mockery and a wrong :
The morning and the evening swiftly blend ;
Soon as the sorrow and the silence end,
A thousand years shall be as yesterday —
    Eternity is long!

SONG PHANTOMS.

They are flitting all about us,
  Fairy forms and faces fair,
Glancing wings of white and silver,
  Spirits not of earth nor air.
    Phantoms of the songs unsung,
    Of unuttered minstrelsy,
    In the noon and in the night
    Still they call to thee and me,
        " Follow ! follow !
" And the song thine own shall be ! "

In the rosy morning sunlight
  Now behold ! thy float and gleam,
Yet shalt thou perceive them nearer
  In the twilight's dusk and dream.
    Softer than all spoken words
    Then their elfin voices ring,
    Sweeter than all chanted hymns
    As they vanish, still they sing —
        " Follow ! follow !
Catch the song upon the wing ! "

Not a brooklet down the valley
  All unhaunted rambles on,
With its limpid wave are blended
    Sacred drops from Helicon.
    And the mountains as they burn
    In the sunset's fiery gold,
    Shine with the mysterious light
    That Parnassus wore of old.
        " Follow ! follow !
And the Muses' shrine behold."

Happy nymph and hapless Echo
  Haunt the wood with ceaseless tone,
Other flowers than famed Narcissus
    Veil a beauty not their own.
    Sighing from the forest bough
    Smiling o'er the rainbow bar,
    Beckoning from the white sea-foam
    Whispering from the vesper star —
        " Follow ! follow !
Bring the spoils of song from far ! "

Oft o'ercome by their enchantment
  We arise and hasten on, —
Follow far through vale and highland
    Till the witching sprite is won.
    Ah ! at touch of mortal hand

See the rainbow plumage fade !
That we sought with rapture sweet
Fails us when our quest is stayed. "
Far we follow,
And we only reach the shade.

Yet with tireless, glad devotion
We go on with eager feet,
For the path is ever starward,
And the wayside bloom is sweet.
Though we gain but broken not
Of the hidden minstrelsy,
Yet we breathe diviner air,
Heavenly heights beyond we see.
We will follow!
Ours at last the song shall be!

UP THE RIVER.

THE barge at sunset left the shore
　With clanging band and banner flying,
Far out at sea we gazed once more,
　The dim, blue line of sky descrying;
Then as we floated up the bay,
We idly watched the sparkling ray
Which on the brightening waters lay,—
　A golden sky, a golden river.

How eerie-like the summer night
　Descends to greet the kindred deep !
Her garments shed a magic light
　As o'er the rippling wave they sweep.
The golden hour of sunset past,
The clouds of amber fading fast,
Grown softer, darker, see at last
　A violet sky, a violet river !

As mists of evening gather dark,
　Diana shows her silver bow,
And now each swift or anchored bark
　Is mirrored in the deep below.

We know not in their ghostly mien
Those dim, white sails that skyward lean;
Real and unreal they hang between
    A shadowy sky and shadowy river.

The wind is down, the tide runs low,
    The barge creeps up the current slowly,
The banks more steep and craggy grow,
    Or darken into woodlands lowly;
And surely yonder peerless star
Shows where the gates of dreamland are!
The pathway brightens near and far
    In sparkling sky and sparkling river.

And now what lights are those that gleam
    From yonder heights with beckoning ray?
Has Norembega's wizard beam
    Shone forth to mock our homeward way?
O no! the lights burn true and fair,
The "welcome home" awaits us there —
Play out, gay band, your sweetest air!
    Good night to starry sky and river!

HAIL AND FAREWELL.

I.

BLOOM, rosy hours, from amber dawn unfold-
  ing
  To noon's imperial splendor, to twilight's
    violet gloom,
All the lost sweetness of forgotten summers
Lives once again in your intense perfume.

Sing, joyous birds! to dreaming sky and
  river,
  Unto the waiting winds a soul melodious
    give;
Till every heart and voice awakes inspired to
  echo
  Your highest note of rapture — "*how sweet
    it is to live!*"

II.

Fade, summer day! unbind thy glowing garland,
  Look from the gate of sunset and smile on
    earth once more;

Fade and farewell; so tranquil be thy slumber,
  The angel stars shall hasten forth thy beauty
    to adore.

Ebb, rapid tide! the dying day reflecting,
  Flow fast, ye golden billows, your ocean
    heaven is nigh,
Melt cloud and wave, in grander deeps dis-
    solving,
  And tell to the departing soul — "*how blest
    it is to die!*"

A SEASIDE PICTURE.

A BROAD, bright bay whose tossing waves
   So sparkle in the sunlight's glare,
   They seem the stolen gems to wear
Of all the nymphs in ocean's caves ;

The foreground rich in woodland shore
   Of odorous cedar, moss grown pine,
   With boughs of lighter green that twine
And bower the velvet pathways o'er.

The distance an enchanting range
   Of island mountains, height on height,
   Where mists of morn and glooms of night
Have wrought a coloring rich and strange, —

A vanishing and mystic hue
   Of blended green and violet dyes,
   And over all such sapphire skies
As Titian's pencil never knew.

Such is the picture I behold,
   And still in every changing light

Some hidden beauty steals in sight,—
A cloud, a shade, a glint of gold.

You ask upon what gallery's wall
  Is this midsummer radiance hung?
  Its name was never said nor sung;
A cottage window frames it all!

ISIS.

Low at her feet I watch and dream,
    She will not lift her veil;
I dimly see a brow sublime
    And features grand and pale,
And feel a mighty heart replies
To all my rapture, or my sighs.

She is so near her breathing falls
    On my attentive ear,
She is so far the twilight stars
    Shine through her mantle clear;
As silent as the grave may be,
And yet the soul of melody!

The lotus trembling on her brow
    Exhales divine perfume,
The mystic splendor of her smile
    Pervades my narrow gloom.
The dearth of solitary hours
She answers with a thousand flowers.

Oppressed with haunting, hindering cares
  My heart rebels at fate.
She stoops to me, and lo! I share
  Her own imperial state.
I glide without my prison bars
And walk with her the path of stars!

Forever sorrowful in death,
  Forever glad in birth,
Her face the glory of the skies,
  Her steps the bloom of earth —
As Nature's self, the fallen, the free,
O Isis, I interpret thee!

LOTUS-EATING.

THESE perfect days were never meant
    For toil of hand or brain,
But for such measureless content
    As heeds no loss nor gain ;
Close held to Nature's flowery breast
In deep midsummer rest.

Within this woodland shade I feel
    The life of wind and tree ;
Soft odors, tremulous boughs reveal
    Untutored ecstasy ;
The wild bird's drowsy warble seems
My own voice heard in dreams !

And yonder azure mountain brow
    Against the opal sky,
The river's cool, melodious flow,
    The pine-tree's pensive sigh,
Each utters forth my inmost mood
Of blissful solitude.

That ever daring deeds were done,
   Or fiery flags unfurled,
Is like a tale of glory won
   In some primeval world,
Where under skies of angry hue
Not yet the lotus grew!

O world, to-day in vain you hold
   The glittering branch of palm;
The lotus hath a flower of gold,
   A fruit of heavenly balm,
And underneath the greenwood tree
Are flower and fruit for me.

A SUNSET AT SEAL POINT COTTAGE.

FROM the gray rocks that walled the beach
    We watched the sinking sun,
Till as the last cloud curtain rolled
Across his drooping crown of gold,
    We said " The day is done."

The gateway of the West was closed,
    The King was seen no more;
And in the pensive even-glow
We strayed with tranquil step and slow
    Along the grassy shore.

But as we gazed, the Eastern sky
    Was lighted up anew :
Long bars of gleaming, crystal green
Across the heavens a dazzling sheen
    Of sudden splendor threw.

The waves along the wide-stretched bay
    Awoke as if from sleep,

And trembling in a strange delight,
Repelled the coming gloom of night
And drank the radiance deep.

Then purple banners richly wrought
  With many a golden sign,
Waved glorious o'er the heavenly plain,
And all the billows shone again
  With blazonry divine.

And ever as a brighter hue
  Illumed the sky and flood,
The mountains on the further shore,
A darker, dreamier aspect wore,
  And with us watching stood.

Still flushed the deepening tints, and now
  A lurid lustre came,
And as with sacrificial fire
The orient burned with splendors dire,
  The sea with tossing flame!

And once again a wondrous change —
  For over all the skies
Swift fading as the night came down,
Were leagues of roses, brightly blown,
  Of pure, celestial dyes!

Fast as they bloomed in heaven they she
   Their petals on the sea!
Till in a rosy wave of light
They vanished from our raptured sight,
   A twilight mystery.

Homeward beneath the whispering trees
   We walked and spoke no word;
For we had seen with living eyes,
On sunset sea and sunset skies,
   The glory of the Lord.

BLACK-CAP MOUNTAIN.

By winding paths, through woods of pine
Deep fringed with fragrant fern and vine,

Old mosses gray beneath our feet,
Wild, forest odors strong and sweet,

Brief spaces where a golden rain
Of sunshine sifts, and here again

Intenser glooms of cliff and tree
Whence some lone bird calls plaintively,

Thus on we move, as in a dream,
Nor know which pleasure is supreme,

Till on the mountain's opening height
All senses lose themselves in sight!

Fair, fair the picture we behold!
A long, dim range of mountains rolled

134

Against the soft October sky,
Seem wrapped in contemplation high.

Far-reaching forests stretch below,
Resplendent with autumnal glow

Of fiery colors, and amid
These leagues of shade, bright waters hid,

Clear, lucid lakes that sparkling rest
Like pearls on Nature's drowsy 'reast.

We almost hear the ripples break
On Chimo's lily-spangled lake,

While far off, like a cloud at rest,
We know Katahdin's kingly crest.

The giant shadows bending low
With soft, slow footfall come and go,

Their cool, gray garments trailing wide
Along each billowy mountain side.

No hint of dust or toil to mar
The living picture shows so far;

Though long we gaze, the vision grows
In perfect beauty and repose.

O when from some sublimer height
These earthly scenes are full in sight,

May all our past transfigured lie
So far, so fair, in memory's eye,

The beauty and the bliss alone
Still visible, and still our own.

RIVERSIDE.

In the house which is my own,
  Though no living eye can read
  The invisible title deed
Which makes it mine alone, —

In the room where my heart and I
  In still communion sit,
  Though as in and out we flit
None heed us passing by, —

I look from the windows three,
  And pictures manifold
  Of the new and of the old
With tireless gaze I see.

The river, near and deep,
  With such endless music flows
  That into my thought it grows,
And I hear it in my sleep.

The trees that o'er it bend,
  Though rugged, old, and gray,

I have talked with day by day,
With each as with a friend.

And yonder far-off range
    Of hills have said to me
    In each change of destiny,
"Behold! we never change."

I have lifted up mine eyes
    And drank their deep repose;
    I have shared the calm which flows
Both from the earth and skies.

From this window I have seen
    Sunsets of pomp untold,
    Islands of rose uprolled
From lakes of luminous sheen.

And after the sunset, far
    In the blue halls of the sky
    I have seen the young moon lie
In her cradle rocked by a star.

Again and oft again
    From yonder window wide,
    I have seen her like a bride
Walk heaven's resplendent plain.

Then the river in its dream
  Was changed to a bridge of light,
  And plume and banner white
Passed over its brilliant beam.

All this may strangers see;
  Yet other sights remain,
  Which shall be sought in vain,
For they only come to me.

The Indian's evening blaze
  Beneath yon broad armed pine,
  For me alone shall shine
Out of remembered days.

The true friend's signal light
  From the home across the way,
  Shall burn to life's last day,
Steadfast and strong and bright.

And if I look no more
  At these pictures far and near,
  Within are scenes as dear,
And I view them o'er and o'er.

For my shadow-sister stands
  In the door, and her sweet, dead eyes

Are filled with a sad surprise
As she touches me with her hands.

"Here I was wont to come,"
She sighs; "in the nights so still
I have wandered here at will:
Oh, is not this thy home?"

And phantom children glide
Across the fireside glow;
Their pale lips murmur low,
"Here we were born, — and died."

Nearer the voices come,
The faces grow more fair;
The loved and lost are there,
For to them it is my home.

O phantoms pass not by!
O river and moaning trees,
My answer is on the breeze,
In the gloaming "Here am I!"

None knows as I have known
The house by the river side,
Nor years nor space divide
The spirit from its own.

TO BEETHOVEN.

I HEAR the voice of thy great, pensive soul,
    In the deep shadow of this summer night,
While far sea waves accordant anthems roll
    From their unfathomed fountains of delight.
I hear thy voice and all my heart is still;
    Hushed in the presence of thy gift divine,
I dream that notes from God's eternal hill,
    From harps that in His awful presence shine,
        Have floated from on high
To sing with Night her vesper hymn of glory,
    But while I listen, lo! it passes by
And leaves me musing o'er thy mournful story.

Thou wast a High Priest of the human heart!
    Holy of Holies was unveiled to thee,
Which thou didst enter in and reverently
    Make all its mysteries of thy theme a part.
All longings for the infinite good unknown,
    And tears for broken idols left behind,
All hopes for buds of beauty yet unblown,
    And deeper yearnings still in shadow shrined,

All the unspoken pain
Or gladness that within the spirit slumbers,
   All that the Poet strives to reach in vain,
'T was thine to utter forth in perfect numbers.

Master of all the spirit's richest deeps!
   Of human nature's grandest, holiest part,
Blessed wast thou in uttering what the heart
   From all the world in sacred stillness keeps!
O blessed is the soul where Genius lives!
   All suffering is a veilèd joy to him;
To his rich life all earthly anguish gives
   A midnight glory, beautiful and dim.
      Out from that midnight calm
Thy gifted spirit's voice serenely flowing,
   Breathes o'er the world's heart like a golden
      psalm,
Sweeter and sadder still forever growing.

FROM ROME.

HERE lies a spray of maiden-hair,
    Tossed over ocean's wintry foam,
A fairy fern, so light, so fair,
    It grew, for me, in Rome!

Day after day with sinking heart
    I saw my summer treasures go,
The last bright leaves in flame depart,
    The dead earth draped in snow.

While all unseen, unknown to me,
    Italia's airs of balmy blue
This leaflet ripened tenderly,
    And hid from heedless view.

No step but thine, Beloved, near
    The fated loveliness might stray,
No eyes to me less true and dear,
    Perceive the emerald spray.

And yesterday, while fierce and fast
    Midwinter raged along the land,

143

Safe borne across the waves, at last
It lay within my hand.

O fairy token! I can see
The ruin old and rich in fame,
Where late my friend remembered me,
And softly spoke my name.

The sculptured fountain's snowy fall,
The rustle of the olive leaves,
The stained and broken marble, — all
My quickened sight perceives.

And more, far more, O friend of mine,
This dear Italian floweret brings,
It is a promise and a sign
Even of immortal things.

Thus all unseen, while earthly skies
Grow dark, and earthly summers flee,
In Heaven's own clime some glad surprise
Unfolds for thee and me.

OBERAMMERGAU.

THE hamlet is in shadow, yet the light
  Clings to the cross on yonder summit hoary,
And wide along the hillside seems to fall
  A benediction and a vesper glory.
Surely some radiant Presence hovering there,
With shining arms uplifted, calls to prayer!
And unseen choristers glide to and fro,
Under the lindens, when the sun is low.

Flame, mountain cross, in the departing day!
  Glow in the sunrise with a rosy splendor!
An altar-fire to which the hills bow down,
  And the hushed valleys meek devotion render.
The world grows cold with unbelief, but here
The Christ of Calvary is ever near,
And beautiful with a perpetual youth
Blooms simple Faith around immortal Truth.

145

WHAT CHEER?

The daylight is dying; how weary and wan
  It sinks to its sleep on the sea's purple breast!
As its last robe of beauty is folded away,
  One funeral star rises out of the west.
What cheer, prophet star, that with sweet, human
    eye
Beamest down on this sad world so pityingly?
Thou dost read all the mysteries of silence and
    night,
And each shadow is changed in thy magical
    light.
        O hear!
Did an angel answer, or was it the star
That wafted a voice through the silence afar?
"Good cheer, doubting spirit! the red rose of
    dawn
On the breast of the desolate midnight is born;
        Good cheer!"

To the muffled music of wind and of rain
  The dreary November is passing away.

There is gloom on the forest, the hill, and the
    plain,
  And wild ocean foams like a lion at bay.
Weary year, dying year, let it haste to the tomb,
All its beauty is vanished, its strength and its
    bloom:
Who would keep the pale spectre a guest at his
    hearth?
But what cheer for the heart as it fades from the
    earth?
        O hear!
With its utterance low comes that voice from on
    high,
Giving back to my sighing its blessed reply —
"Good cheer! a new life, a new year shall arise
And fill with its glory the earth and the skies!
        Good cheer!"

Answer once more, O thou beautiful star!
  Chase the last doubt from my spirit away,
I too, like the year, must be gathered to dust,
  My youth in its brightness shall fade like the
    day.
Must my beautiful visions lie down with me?
Must my hopes in the grave bear me company?
And all that I yearned for of glory and bloom,
Go out, like a lamp, in the chill of the tomb?

O hear!
Whether angel answered, or only a star,
Of joy and of promise the tidings are!
" For thy feet there are paths which **no** mortal
hath trod,
For thy hope there is room in the gardens of God!
Good cheer!"

A VIGIL.

All-Souls' Day! Where have I heard or read
  An old-time legend, sad and sweet,
That to-night return the remembered dead
  And walk among us with shadowy feet?
The watcher heedeth no sight nor sound,
But till dawn is breaking they throng around.

Beloved! thou hast been gone from me
  A year and a day. I will watch to-night.
My door shall be left ajar for thee;
  I will brighten my fire and trim my light,
And musing softly on other days,
Vigil I'll keep by the midnight blaze.

Are there untold joys in those realms above,
  With whose meaning mortals may vainly cope?
Blooms there a sweeter rose than love?
  Sings there a happier bird than hope?
Was the waking all that thy dream foretold
Of palm and palace and gates of gold?

149

Thou didst love me truly, I doubt it not.
   To part was bitter though silent pain;
In that far-off realm am I yet forgot?
   Is mourning empty and memory vain?
Hark! was that a whisper, so soft, so near?
It is but the sighing wind I hear.

How fair to me was thy fading face,
   Touched with a tender and tranquil glow
Heaven had lent thee its promised grace —
   A coming rapture was on thy brow.
Thy smile — ah! what shines so within the door?
Only the moonlight just touching the floor.

We were happy, love, in those summer days,
   The days of sunshine so bright, so long,
Pleasant our walks by the flowery ways,
   Sweet the communing by word and song.
Listen! — O melody come once again!
All silent. I must have been dreaming, then.

I hear the wash of the troubled tide
   As it breaks on the cold, unheeding shore,
The elm trees grieve by the river side,
   And the murmuring pines reply "no more."
Low in the east hangs the star of dawn.
Has the angel visitant come and gone?

Surely one moment she stooped to see
  The light on my hearth, and her glance was
    kind.
Such presence veiled from our sight must be;
  The dead are not faithless, though we are blind.
In the light of the same undying love
We watch below, and they watch above.

INDIAN SUMMER.

WHEN the hunter's moon is waning,
  And hangs like a crimson bow,
And the frosty fields of morning
  Are white with a phantom snow;
Who then is the beautiful spirit,
  That wanders, smiles, and grieves
Along the desolate hill-sides,
  And over the drifted leaves?

She has strayed from the far-off dwelling
  Of forgotten Indian braves,
And stolen wistfully earthward
  Over the path of graves;
She has left the cloudy gateway
  Of the hunting-grounds ajar,
To follow the trail of the summer
  Toward the morning star.

There 's a rustle of soft, slow footsteps,
  The toss of a purple plume,
And the glimmer of golden arrows
  Athwart the hazy gloom.

'Tis the smoke of the happy wigwams
   That reddens our wintry sky,
The scent of unfading forests
   That is dreamily floating by.

O shadow sister of summer!
   Astray from the world of dreams,
Thou wraith of the bloom departed,
   Thou echo of springtide streams,
Thou moonlight and starlight vision
   Of a day that will come no more,
Would that our love might win thee
   To dwell on this stormy shore!

But the roaming Indian goddess
   Stays not for our tender sighs;
She has heard the call of her hunters
   Beyond the sunset skies!
By her beaming arrows stricken
   The last leaves fluttering fall,
With a sigh and a smile she has vanished,
   And darkness is over all.

BANGOR CENTENNIAL HYMN.

1769–1869.

God of our days! Thy guiding power
    Sustained the lonely pioneer
Who first, amid the forest shades,
    His evening camp-fire kindled here.
To thee a welcome sacrifice,
Its smoke ascended to the skies.

God of the years! As summers fled,
    Within the wild, new homes were reared,
New gardens bloomed, new altars flamed,
    And songs of praise the Sabbaths cheered,
Until the fair, young city stood
Gem of the eastern solitude.

God of the centuries! To-day
    A hundred years their tale have told,
And lingering in their solemn shade
    We listen to the days of old.
To us how vast the centuries flight,
To Thee as watches in the night.

154

God of eternity! Thy hand
  To nobler hills has beckoned on
The fathers, who by many toils
  For us this pleasant dwelling won.
With them hereafter may we raise
Celestial cities to Thy praise!

WINTER OUR GUEST.

He is come, the guest unbidden,
Guest unwelcome, sure to tarry.
While we lingered in the doorway,
Saying farewells fond and tender
To the dark-browed Indian summer,
Sunburned, beautiful enchantress,
While we watched her slow departure
With regretful, pensive feeling,
Lo! a chariot rolling swiftly
Brought a traveller to our door!

Stern old Winter! See he enters
As if sure of right unquestioned,
Heeding not our gloomy faces,
Our half-uttered salutations;
On the threshold waits a moment,
Doffs and shakes his cloak of ermine,
And the air is filled with downy
Flakes that fall in feathery flight.

Once within, with steady footsteps
To the very shrine and altar

Of our household he advances.
Underneath his shaggy forehead,
Grim and stern with many a wrinkle,
Gleam his eyes so cold and steely.
Closer cling the little children
To our side, and look with timid
Glances on the strange intruder,
Shrinking from his icy hand.

Sometimes when the windows darken
With the clouds of snow descending,
When the wind escaped from prison,
Holds a revel with the snow-wraith,
Then the frown of some old viking
Darkens on his rugged features.
And as nearer, wilder, louder
Rolls the battle wave of tempest,
Fierce and fiercer grows his visage,
And in undertones he mutters
Of the storms of all the ages,
As he holds unseen communion
With the spirits of the air.

But he is not always sullen,
Brooding over thoughts revengeful;
When the early sunlight glitters
On the snow-fields, heavy laden

With a magic, midnight harvest —
When the trees which bare and ghastly
Bent before the evening tempest,
In the morning stand transfigured
Into lovely flowering almonds,
Every branch a mass of blossom
White as down and pure as crystal,
Then the aged brow is softened,
And the voice prophetic utters
Promise of a fruitful burden
To the glistening fields and boughs.

And again when bells are chiming
In the moonlight and the starlight
Of the saintly Christmas even,
When the lights in every window
Show sweet faces bright with pleasure, —
All the brightness is reflected
In his eyes, and fearless fingers
Twine his hoary locks with holly.
Then beneath the lighted fir-tree,
Brilliant with a fairy fruitage,
Sits he like a king, dispensing
Royal gifts with royal smiles.

Long he tarries, but he listens
When the days are growing longer,

Listens till he hears the laughter,
Rippling in the sunny distance,
Of the winsome April maiden.
As we spring up in our gladness
Echoing back her song of welcome,
He will gaze into our faces
As if fain awhile to linger.
But as nearer comes the dancing,
Mirthful, musical young goddess,
With the scent of early violets
Shed from her sun-lighted tresses,
He will totter to the threshold,
Looking, lingering, O so wistful!
Till with late, repentant kindness,
As he sadly is departing,
We will touch his cold, wan fingers,
Saying softly — " *Friend, farewell!* "

IMMORTELLES.

HERE bloom no flowers. The river glides
Beneath the shade of sombre pines,
The bank is rich with purpling vines
That lean to watch the changing tides.
But garden beds and walks for me
Have lost their olden witchery,
Since, trusting they would spring again
Beneath the sunshine and the rain,
     I planted deep my Immortelles.

And that was long ago. They sleep
Unmindful of caressing dews,
Of all the kindred blossom hues
That round their place of slumber creep.
The west-wind sighs amid the leaves,
The wild-bird answering, sweetly grieves,
They hear nor heed ; alike unstirred
By tenderest voice of wind or bird,
     They sleep, my spotless Immortelles.

At times when down the darkened sky
Rushes the storm on angry wing,

When all the leaves are shuddering
And the torn blossoms sob and sigh,
I think of them, — in earth's fond breast
Held in such still and perfect rest,
And I am comforted to know
O'er them no blighting wind can blow,
    No ruin reach my Immortelles!

The days are long, but calm and strong
Will Love's own presence on them wait,
And fear no league with Death nor Fate.
Sure is the joy though tarrying long.
Each year new promise seems to bring,
New signals of eternal spring.
Perhaps ere Summer fades my eyes
Will see my flowers of Paradise —
    Will look upon my Immortelles.

The hour will come; a twilight gloom,
With flowers upon the pillow laid
By hands that tremble, half-afraid
Of the strange stillness in my room.
O friends, fear not! My eyes will be
No longer holden. I shall see
In all their passion of perfume,
In all their brilliancy of bloom,
    My own, my deathless Immortelles.

CONSOLATION.

NATURE is not pitiless!
  When upon some sudden woe
  Mornings glitter, sunsets glow
As in glad unconsciousness,

When upon our dead delight
  Sweet winds play and roses bloom,
  And we seem to have no room
For our sorrow, and no right—

Then, ah! then could we but know
  From what wealth of bliss eternal
  Nature's joyance, fresh and vernal,
Overflows upon our woe, —

From what opulence of light
  She shines down upon our grief,
  Till in glimpses comes relief
As the star-beams to the night, —

From all doubting we should cease,
  Knowing that our faltering glance

Faints and falls in the expanse
Of a universe of peace.

Mother Nature, fair and grand,
    Mocks us not, but round us throwing
    Her warm arms, with love o'erflowing
Bids us wait and understand.

Then we see that air and sky
    Throb with beauteous, boundless life,
    Winds and woods and waves are rife
With unfailing melody.

Every discord of to-day,
    Ocean's moan or tempest's jar,
    Ere it can the chorus mar,
Drowned in music dies away.

And we dimly feel and know
    Something deep within keeps time
    To the wonderful glad rhyme
Of the ages as they flow.

Something mightier than pain,
    Heaven's own echo in the heart,
    Bids us rise and take our part
In the song of life again.

Therefore Nature, loving Sage,
  Smiles the brighter when we weep,
  Knowing that we can but keep
Our eternal heritage.

SONNETS.

165

SONNETS.

ORIENT TO OCCIDENT.

MINE is the elder right, the ancient throne,
  The purple of the centuries is mine!
  The birthplace of the race, its earliest shrine
Was to my ever blooming gardens known.
Upon my dewy sunrise slopes has grown
  The tree of Knowledge, of whose fruit divine
  Have feasted bard and sage, a noble line, —
The fountains of all history are my own.
My fields are white with harvests of brave deeds
  And rich with blood of heroes, and the air
  Is sweet with songs of victory heard afar;
Mine are the elder gods, the cradle creeds
Of the wild north, the fervent south, and fair
  On my horizon rose the Bethlehem Star.

167

OCCIDENT TO ORIENT.

WEAR thy proud honors still, imperial East,
    Thou warrior of the ages! but for me
    A new day dawns, — a fairer history
Than ever graced the scroll of seer or priest;
For Liberty from ancient thrall released
    Calls to the nations over land and sea,
    To the oppressed who should be strong and
        free,
To sit with her at a perpetual feast.
My poets sing no more of battling foes,
    But in this true Valhalla of the West
    Shall god-like wisdom, arts divine, increase;
And here the star that on Judea rose,
    Shall light the long-sought gardens of the
        Blest, —
The home of nations and the throne of Peace.

THE SEVEN DAYS.

I.

DAY OF THE MOON.

DIANA, sister of the sun, thy ray
  Governs these opening hours. The world is
    wide;
We know not what new evil may betide
This six days' journey; by what unknown
    way
We come at last unto the royal day
  Of prophecy and promise. O preside,
  Propitious, and our doubting footsteps guide
Onward and sunward. Long in shadows gray
We have but slumbered; hidden from our
    view
  Knowledge and wisdom in unfruitful night.
But if upon the dawn's unfolding blue
  Thy hand to-day our destiny must write,
Once more our outer, inner life renew
  With Heaven's first utterance, "*Let there be
    light.*"

II.

DAY OF THE WAR-GOD.

Fear not, O soul, to-day! the kingly Mars
  Leads on the hours, a brave and warlike train,
  Fire in his glance and splendor in his reign,
From the first glitter through the sunrise bars
Till his red banner flames among the stars.
  Thou, too, go forth, and fully armed maintain
  Duty and right: the hero is not slain,
Though pierced and wounded in a hundred
    wars.
For daring deeds are deathless. He alone
  Is victor, who stays not for any doom
Foreshadowed; utters neither sigh nor moan,
  Death-stricken, but right onward, his fair plume
  Scorched in the battle-flame, through smoke
    and gloom
Strikes for the right, nor counts his life his own.

III.

DAY OF ODIN.

The mighty Odin rides abroad, and earth
  Trembles and echoes back his ghostly sigh,—
  More deep than thought, more sad than memory.
The very birds sing low in timid mirth,

For in the forest sudden gusts have birth,
  And harsh against the pale appealing sky
  Ascends his ravens' melancholy cry.
Peace be with Odin! Of his ancient worth
Many and grand the tales we will repeat,
  For sacred memories to these hours belong.
But yesterday with reckless speed our feet
  Dared the bold height. With spirit no less
      strong
To-day step softly. After battle's heat
  Warriors and wars are only themes for song.

IV.

DAY OF THOR.

White-robed, white-crowned, and borne by steeds
    snow-white,
  The Thunderer rolls along the echoing skies.
  No hour is this to dream of past emprise,
Or with old runes the memory to delight.
The mountain tops with prophet beams are
    bright,
  The eagle soars aloft with jubilant cries —
  Thou, too, unto the hills lift up thine eyes,
To some new throne these sacred signs invite.
Learn thy own strength; and if some secret sense
  Of power untried pervades thy low estate,

Bend thy soul's purest, best intelligence
   To seek the mastery of time and fate.
Courage and deathless hope and toil intense
   Are the crown-jewels of the truly great.

V.

DAY OF LOVE AND PLEASURE.

In the world garden, walled with living green,
   The foam-born goddess of delight to-day
   Plucks glorious blossoms for her own array.
Poppies and myrtle in her wreath are seen,
And roses, bending o'er her brow serene,
   Blush to perceive she is more fair than they.
   Sweet grasses at her feet their odors lay,
And doves, low warbling, hover o'er their
     queen.
In this brief life shall ever toil and care
   Hold fast our wishes? Earth's bewildering
     bowers,
Her streams melodious and her woodlands
     fair,
   Are palaces for gods. The world is ours!
Beauty and love our birthright, — we will
     share
   The sunshine and the singing and the
     flowers.

VI.

DAY OF SATURN.

Though bright with jewels, and with garlands
    dressed,
  The bloom decays, the world is growing old.
  Lost are the days when peaceful Saturn told
The arts to men, and cheered their toil or rest
With eloquence divine. The Olympian guest
  Took with him in his flight the age of gold.
  Westward through myriad centuries has rolled
The ceaseless pilgrimage, the hopeless quest
For the true Fatherland. Through weary years
  What if some rainbow glory spans the gloom,
Some strong, sweet utterance the wayside cheers,
  Or gladness opens like a rose in bloom?
Step after step the fatal moment nears,
  Earth for new graves is ever making room.

VII.

DAY OF THE SUN.

Thou glorious Sun! illumining the blue
  Highway of Heaven! to thy triumphant rays
  The earth her shadow yields, the hill-tops
    blaze, —
Up lifts the mist, up floats the morning dew.

Old things ɩre passed away, the world is new !
  Labor is changed to rest, and rest to praise !
  Past are the weary heights, the stormy days, —
The eternal future breaks upon our view.
Last eve we lingered, uttering our farewe'
  But lo! One met us in the early light
Of this divinest morn.   The tale He tells
  Transfigures life and opens Heaven to sight.
Bring altar flowers ! lilies and asphodels !
  Sing jubilates !   *There is no more night.*

LONGFELLOW.

WHITHER, beloved spirit, art thou fled?
  Couldst thou not linger with thine own, at least
  Till the glad singing at thy birthday feast
Had died away? Still fresh upon thy head
The perfume of love's latest wreath is shed.
  Thy new year's daybreak reddens in the east,
  The warm air throbs with music not yet
    ceased —
Why stand the minstrels hushed around thy bed?

Falls thy own whisper from the fields divine —
  "There is no death!" The angel Israfil,
  Flashing swift splendor on our startled gaze,
But crowned and led thee home. No word nor
    sign
We need to know thou art a poet still,
And sweeter for thy songs are heaven's high-
    ways.
175

VICTORIA.

THE sovereign lady of dominions grand,
　　Flower of a chivalrous and noble age,
　　Hers is to-day a matchless heritage.
The sceptre held within her gentle hand
Shines with unsullied beam; a starry band
　　Of bards and sages write her history's page,
　　While boundless love and loyalty presage
Joy to her banners upon sea and land.

But we, in this free land across the sea,
　　Find in her fair and gracious womanhood
　　A higher royalty. No more alone
Can England claim her; she has risen to be
　　Queen among women. Simply great and good,
　　In the world's heart Victoria has her throne.

TO THE RAINBOW.

O Iris, bringing balm for summer's tears,
   So lightly stepping down thy bridge of rose,
   I know not why my spirit drinks repose
Soon as thy footfall the horizon nears.
Spell-bound I watch the crimson shaded piers,
   As arch by arch the blooming pathway grows,
   And where the warmest tint of color shows,
I trace thy trailing garment. Sighs and fears
Are vanished; in a long and ardent gaze
   Thy steps I follow down the heavenly slope.
Iris! be mine thy message! Let thy rays
   Write out how I with destiny may cope.
Ah! spanned with light would be all coming
     days,
   Could I but read thy oracle of hope.

THE MAGIC FLUTE.

A FLUTE upon the water! and I lean
  At the broad window in the moonlight clear,
  That low, wild, rippling melody to hear.
A white batteau with dripping oar is seen
Skimming the moonbeam path of silver sheen,
  And now a shadow into shadows drear
  It vanishes, yet to my longing ear
The melody floats back, a sound serene
Endowed by night with sweetness not its own.
  O happy player! drifting down the tide,
Half of thy music's charm thou hast not known;
  With me alone its magic shall abide —
For fairy lips with thine the strain have blown,
  And love's lost whisper in the echo sighed!

178

MIDNIGHT.

At midnight I behold, far past her prime,
　The pallid moon slow rising in the sky,
A queen discrowned, her pomp and pride past
　　　by,
Pacing a joyless palace; yet sublime
In desolation, mindful of the time
　When reigned full-orbed her loveliness on
　　　high,
　And planets paled before her majesty.
Now dumb and dread the hour; not even a
　　chime
Of elfin music.　Flower and leaf and bough
　Dream in the marble moonlight.　Cold and
　　　bright
The river sleeps, its tide at flood, and slow
　Soft clouds like phantoms gliding into sight
Linger beneath the stars' funereal glow.
　The day is dead — thou art its spectre, Night!

179

DAYBREAK.

WHEN out of heaven steals the first ray of dawn
And wanders, lost, in labyrinths of night,
The wakeful robin notes with quickened sight
The half-affrighted herald of the morn.
Softly he trills to cheer the beam forlorn,
And others hear the signal, until bright
Approach the bolder ranks of orient light,
And night is of its shadowy terror shorn.
Withdraw, O Hesper! silver-mantled priest!
And quench with haste thy taper's dying ray:
For now with sudden hush the birds have ceased,
Rich banners float o'er the horizon gray,
And past his fire-plumed escort, in the east
Rides the anointed King, Imperial Day!

180

FRIENDSHIP.

It matters not if no more face to face
  I look on thee, my friend. Though sweet
    indeed
  To clasp thy hand in mine, there is no need ;
Our perfect friendship knows no time nor place.
Heart reaches heart across unmeasured space,
  Soul touches soul from ruder contact freed ;
    Ours is one hope, one life-work and one creed,
One destiny the flying moments trace.
The shadow of thy grief cannot depart
  Till it is fallen on me ; thy new delight
    Flashes swift radiance over land and sea.
Such friendship is an Eden for the heart,
  In which it grows to blossom without blight,
    Gives itself wholly and is wholly free.

THE FLOWER PAINTER.

I.

She learned the dearest haunts in vale and wild
  Of summer's fairy nurslings. In her eyes
  The opening buds beheld with glad surprise
Such loving recognition, that they smiled
Ecstatic welcome. Nature pleased and mild
  Guided her hand to seek the precious dyes
  Kept hidden since the loss of Paradise,
And with pure sense and spirit undefiled
She shared the secret with each flower that grew.
  Beneath her touch the treasures manifold
Of fading summers lived in beauty new.
  The rose with glowing blush its story told,
  Violet and heart's-ease breathed in blue and
    gold,
And spotless lilies sparkled with the dew.

II.

And then her hand grew weary ; full and deep
The cup of life and love, and beauty's ray
Crowned her young brow as on her bridal day.
Not hers the doom to linger and to weep,
Nor feel the winds of stormy anguish sweep.

Within her eyes strange, wistful shadows lay;
The pencil from her light grasp dropped away,
And while the flowers slept, she too fell asleep.

"But summer days are come; will she return
Whose step a thousand blossoms yearn to greet?"
O questioning flowers! she has gone hence to
        learn
If in that land your own life is complete;
If heavenward borne on wings of odor sweet
Ye, too, in hues of deathless beauty burn.

EBB AND FLOW.

My river! Thou art like the poet's soul,
  Where tides of song perpetual ebb and flow.
  Like thine the current of his life runs low
At times, his visions suffer loss and dole,
And sunken griefs break through the waters
    shoal.
  Then while despair is tossing to and fro
  His stranded hope, a breath begins to blow
From the great sea! With rising swell and roll
The waves of inspiration lift and float
  His being into broad and full expanse.
Now rocks his fancy like an airy boat
  On wreathed billows ; his impassioned glance
Little of cloud or reef or wreck will note,
  On the high tide of song in blissful trance.

HAPPINESS.

Long time I looked in every passing face
  In search of happiness, — the signal light
  Of an interior flame, — the blossom-bright
Midsummer of the soul, — but found no trace
Till yesterday in a most lonely place,
  One on whose heart had fallen woful blight,
  Said to me — " In the heaviness of night
I can *remember* Joy's supremest grace!"

O Fortunate! Once to have felt the glow
  Of full delight; to bear within the breast
  Even the ashes of life's perfect bloom.
Earth gives no more; the happiness we know
Is veiled when with us, — in the vanished guest
  We first perceive an angel's fleeting plume.

185

SOUNDS FROM HOME.

WHY, when sweet sounds are borne upon the air,
  Doth such a homesick longing, not all pain,
  A gladness greater than we can sustain,
Enthrall the sense, until we seem to share
Joys of some higher realm, we know not where?
  Doth then the spirit for a moment gain
  Ascendency o'er powers that long have lain
Dormant beneath a load of earthly care,
And recognize the sounds and sighs of home?
  O Melody! the subtle power is thine
  The inmost deeps of memory to reach,
The heights supreme of hope, till we are come
  Near the soul's fatherland: we touch the line
  Beyond which music is the only speech.

186

FAR AND NEAR.

THIS little picture from across the sea
   Shows me a foreign city's stately square,
   A sculptured column piercing the blue air
Within its midst, and fountains dashing free
On either side, while many a bowery tree
   Shades the wide pathways from the summer's
      glare.
Princes of art and song have wandered there
In years gone by; yet is it more to me
That in yon olden palace, looking down
   Upon the winged marbles, dwells to-day
The beautiful companion of my youth,
Who, roving through the fair, historic town,
   Thinks of me still, and wafts from far away
The blest aroma of a warm heart's truth.

FOREST WORSHIP.

We stood beneath the shadow of the wood
  In Nature's own Cathedral. High in air
  Hemlock and pine tree met in arches fair,
And at our feet, as if they understood
The forest's Sabbath's hushed, expectant mood,
  The waves flowed back, till in the mid-day
     glare
  The gray rocks stood like monks with foreheads
    bare.
Suddenly from the inner solitude
  A choir of sparrows in long, sweet refrain
  Intoned a litany. There was no room
  For priest nor psalm nor any spoken word,
For here the Spirit often sought in vain
  Brooded at peace, and in the tranquil gloom
  We almost heard the footsteps of our Lord.

ISOLATION.

Most solitary ! This is thy complaint !
   Then teach thy brooding spirit to forsake
   Self-contemplation. Rise up and partake
Of Nature's converse. She hath fancies quaint,
Poetic moods, love legends without taint,
   Such as the wild-bird tells by brook and brake,
   Or the white lily dreams upon the lake,
Seen but by cloud and star, a vestal saint.
The forest bud expands in perfect bloom,
   The meadow pool Heaven's starry splendor
      knows !
So thou superior to thy lonely doom,
   May'st win each grace the fleeting hour
      bestows,
Until all redolent of rare perfume
   Thy wilderness shall blossom as the rose.

189

HE loved them, — and what offering more meet
  Wherewith to deck this pleasant, peaceful
    place,
Than flowers, the living language of His grace.
Dearer to Him than incense, for their sweet
Adoring beauty drew His wayworn feet
  To linger near them. For their sake His face
  Grew luminous, though no brief delight could
    chase
That sacred, inner shadow. See Him greet,
  With word and touch the lilies of the field!
  That word has given them subtler power than
    speech,
That touch has made them glorious; and the
    best
  The purest invocations we can yield,
  The praise our faltering accents fail to reach,
We utter in the flowers that he has blest.

STAR SOLITUDE.

I SOMETIMES wonder if yon star of even
  Which has for everlasting ages shone
  Stately and fair on its immaculate throne,
Ever looks forth, with sudden anguish riven,
Into the silver space, reproaching heaven
    That in the very grandeur all its own
    A doom is fixed, to be for aye alone!
Eternal solitude with glory given.

The cottage lamp shines cheerily and strong
  Into the night. It tells of evening mirth,
  Of cradle music by the beaming hearth,
Rest, comfort, pleasure that to Home belong.
But thou, O Radiance! high above the earth,
  Ever and only hearest thine own song!

ST. CECILIA.

WHEN St. Cecilia, soul of song and fire,
    Heard angels sing the numbers which had
      lain
Unutterable within her fervid brain,
Heart-sick with hopeless, passionate desire,
In fragments at her feet she dashed her lyre!
    Broken, it could no longer mock her pain,
    Nor voice so ill the sweet, ideal strain
Which rang melodious from the heavenly choir.
O sad saint! was it not enough to know
    Such music *lived*, though still beyond thy
      reach?
And wiser far, with tender touch and slow,
    Thy instrument's mute helplessness to teach?
Content if ever from its strings should flow
    Some syllables of that celestial speech!